Change

From Jacob To Israel

Kevin L. Adams, Sr., and **Craig L. Ervin**

This book is designed to provide accurate and authoritative information regarding the subject matter covered. This information is given with the understanding that neither the author nor LEEDS PRESS CORP is engaged in rendering legal or professional advice. The opinions expressed by the author are not necessarily those of LEEDS PRESS CORP.

Copyright 2024 © Leeds Press Corp

Cover copyright 2024 © Leeds Press Corp

Cover Design by Leeds Graphics.

Written by Bishop Kevin L. Adams, Sr., and Craig L. Ervin.

Edited by Leeds Press Corp, Staff

Leeds Press Corp encourages the right to free expression and the importance of copyright. Copyright aims to encourage authors and artists to produce innovative works that strengthen society. **Change: From Jacob to Israel** is a LEEDS PRESS CORP publication. No part of this publication may be reproduced, stored in a retrieval system, or transmitted by any means, electronic, mechanical, photocopy, recording, or otherwise, without the author's prior permission except as provided by USA copyright law. If you would like permission to use material from the book (other than for review purposes), please contact info@leedspress.com. The opinions expressed by the author are not necessarily those of LEEDS PRESS CORP.

Leedspublishing.com

Twitter.com/leedspresscorp

Instagram.com/leedspresscorp

Facebook.com/leedspresscorp

TABLE OF CONTENTS

CHAPTER 1

The Birth of Change

²¹ Isaac prayed to the LORD for his wife because she was barren. And the LORD granted his prayer, and Rebekah, his wife, conceived. ²² The children struggled together within her, and she said, "If it is thus, why is this happening to me?" So she went to inquire of the LORD. ²³ The LORD said to her, "Two nations are in your womb, and two peoples from within you shall be divided; the one shall be stronger than the other, the older shall serve the younger." ²⁴ When her days to give birth were completed, behold, there were twins in her womb. ²⁵ The first came out red, all his body like a hairy cloak, so they called his name Esau. ²⁶ Afterward, his brother came out with his hand holding Esau's heel, so his name was Jacob. Isaac was sixty years old when she bore them. ²⁷ When the boys grew up, Esau was a skillful hunter, a man of the field, while Jacob was a quiet man, dwelling in tents. ²⁸ Isaac loved Esau because he ate his game, but Rebekah loved Jacob. (**Genesis 25:21-27**).

The history of the world changed forever because Rebekah was thirsty. Years before she prayed for the children, she went to the well for water. One of the themes in the Bible is about meeting a woman at a well.

- The angel of the Lord meets Hagar by a spring of water (**Gen. 16:7**).
- Rebekah meets the servant of Abraham at the well (**Gen. 24:16**).
- Jacob meets Rachel at the well (**Gen. 29:9**).
- Moses meets Zipporah at a well (**Ex. 2:17**).
- Jesus met the woman from Samaria at a well (**John 4:7**).

The story of change will never begin until we become thirsty for change. The thirsty's parched throat and dry lips go to the source and draw water. Rebekah was thirsty for God. When the servant of Abraham came to find a bride for Isaac, Rebekah did not hesitate. She left immediately, said farewell to her family that she would never see again, and traveled to marry a man she had never met. Rebekah became the wife of Isaac and followed Yahweh, the God of Abraham.

Rebekah quenched her thirst for a relationship with God, but her life was still incomplete. She was barren. There are six barren women in the Bible, all connected to the promise of God.

- Sarah was barren (**Gen. 16:1**)
- Rebekah was barren (**25:21**)
- Rachel was barren (**29:31**)
- Hannah was barren (**1 Sam. 1:5**)
- Samson's mother (**Judges 13:2**)
- Elizabeth (**Luke 1:7**)

The theme of barrenness runs through biblical history because redemption and change are beyond man's control. What we cannot do, God does. We are barren, unable to bring life into the world. God brings forth life from barrenness. He is the wellspring of life: The source of new life and new beginnings. We are barren, unable to change on our own. Jesus said, *"apart from me, you can do nothing."* (**John 15:5**). Still, He also said, *"What is impossible for man is possible with God."* (**Luke 18:27**). We are all barren, all of us unable through our own will and own strength to bring true change into our lives and to the world. It is only through the resurrection power of Jesus that we can change.

A barren womb is like a barren tomb. Jesus was dead and placed in the tomb. There was no life in a tomb, *"but God raised him from the dead."* (**Acts 13:30**). The Bible promises us that the same power that raised up Jesus from the dead can bring real change into our lives: *"Just as Christ was raised from the dead by the glory of the Father, we too might walk in newness of life."* (**Rom. 6:4**). Throughout the Bible, God brought forth children from barren women to show us that He can change any situation. He brings life from death, healing from sickness, and joy from sadness. He can break any habit, heal any disease, and change any life as surely as Jesus Christ rose from the dead.

Rebekah had a relationship with God but was barren. She needed a significant change in her life, as without a new generation, the promise made to Abraham would end with Isaac. It was her destiny to bear a son who would inherit Yahweh's blessing, but she remained barren month after month, year after year. Then, Isaac prayed, and Rebekah became pregnant with the promise of the Lord. Prayer is an absolutely essential element for real change in our lives, and God always answers prayers. However, His responses may not always align with our expectations. Sometimes, an answer to prayer brings more questions.

Complications

Rebekah began experiencing complications during her pregnancy. Although she had received her miracle, a significant problem arose. The scripture notes, "The children struggled together within her, and she said, 'If it is thus, why is this happening to me?'" The term "struggle" in this context is defined as "to crush" or "to oppress." (This word is used in **Judges 9:53** when a woman dropped a large stone on the head of Abimelech, and it crushed his skull open.) Rebekah turned to the Lord for understanding because she knew God had answered her prayer for children, yet the turmoil within her was overwhelming. She asked the Lord, "If this is your will and gift to me, why does it feel like I am being torn up inside?"

When you pray to God for change, He responds with blessings and challenges. Change is painful, and Rebekah's experience reflects this. She questioned God about her suffering, and while God provided explanations, He did not alleviate her pain. Many people abandon God's plan for their lives due to the discomfort and challenges of change. They forfeit what God has initiated within them because it is difficult or inconvenient. Real change often entails real pain. Rebekah was pregnant with a word from God before she could give birth to His purpose. Pregnancy itself is challenging—it stretches you and burdens you with the weight of new life. Do not let the pain of change deter you from the change process.

God revealed to Rebekah that there was purpose in her pain, saying, "*There are two nations inside you...*" The prayer that resolved her barrenness also initiated a conflict. Rebekah was expecting twins, and these twins were in discord. The battle within her was due to the two contrasting natures striving for dominance. There was an Esau inside Rebekah, who showed little regard for God and lived by the desires of the flesh. Simultaneously, there was a Jacob who sought nothing but God's promise and blessing. Two individuals representing two nations, embodying two natures, destined to be in perpetual conflict until one prevails. The apostle Paul talks about this warfare of two "laws" within us. "*For I delight in the law of God, in my inner being, but I see in my members another law waging war against the law of my mind and making me captive to the law of sin that dwells in my members."* (**Rom. 7:22,23**). Paul says he wants to change, to "**do good**," but *"the evil I do not want is what I keep doing."* (**Rom. 7:19**). This is the struggle, the crushing within Rebekah and within us when we try to change our lives. We want to change, but we also do not want to change. These two "**nations**" wage war within us until we are delivered. Paul said, *"Who will deliver me from this body of death? Thanks be unto God through Jesus Christ our Lord."* (**Rom. 7:24, 25**).

The Promise

God promised Rebekah: "*The one shall be stronger than the other, and the older shall serve the younger.*" This highlights the inherent conflict between our sinful nature—a "law" or "nation" within us that opposes God—and the transformative power of following Jesus. When we embrace faith in Jesus, we receive His Spirit, instilling a new "law" and a new nature. This divine transformation makes us a new creation in Christ, fundamentally changing our inner spiritual landscape and redirecting our life's course. *"Therefore, if anyone is in Christ, he is a new creation. The old has passed away, behold, the new has come."* (**2 Cor. 5:17**). The power of the Spirit of Jesus in us overcomes the power of the old sin nature. "The older shall serve the younger." The promise of God to Rebekah was that the warfare within her had purpose and destiny. Jacob, the younger one, would win over Esau, the older one.

The Bible explicitly states that the promise to Rebekah signifies God's choice of Jacob. The Apostle Paul explains, "When Rebekah conceived children...though they were not yet born and had done nothing either good or bad—so that God's purpose of election might proceed, not by works but by Him who calls—she was told.", *"The older shall serve the younger."* (**Romans 9:11,12**). God chose Jacob. God called Jacob. This choosing and calling are encapsulated in the word of promise. This word of promise signifies that before Jacob was carried in the womb of Rebekah, he was carried in the heart of God. This word also indicates that before Jacob was born, he *"had done nothing either good or bad,"* and he was already chosen by God to prevail. Jacob did not earn or deserve the promise of God; similarly, if you do not earn it through your actions, you cannot lose it through your actions either. The promise of God is that your past cannot stop you because you were chosen to win.

The Bible says, *"... He chose us in Him before the foundation of the world, that we should be holy and blameless before Him in love..."*. (**Eph. 1:4**). When God chose us in Christ before the foundation of the world, He declared a word of choosing about us, just as He did for Jacob. Before time began, God proclaimed a word of promise concerning our role in His plan. Jacob was called and chosen by God before he ever did anything *"good or bad."* The reason we can change, the reason we can "be holy and blameless before Him in love," is not rooted in our own strength but in the power of His promise.

Before we ever made mistakes or even recognized our need for change, God had already spoken a promise to us. It doesn't matter what we've done, what others say about us, or how often we've failed. What truly matters is that God has chosen us and called us with a word of promise.

The power of God, manifest through His word, enables the promised change. Just as Jacob was transformed into Israel, so too can we, the "**children of Jacob**," change because God has spoken, and His words will come to pass. *"So shall my word be that goes out of my mouth; it shall not return to me empty, but it shall accomplish that which I purpose and shall succeed in the thing for which I sent it."* (**Isaiah 55:11**). The apostle Peter said, *"...He has granted to us his precious and great promises, so that through them you may become partakers of the divine nature..."* (**2 Peter 1:4**). It is the word of promise from God that enables Rebekah to endure her pregnancy and the associated pain because she holds onto the assurance that "the one shall be stronger than the other."

When God speaks a word, it becomes a reality. And God said, *'Let there be light, and there was light."* (**Gen. 1:3**). This same power works in us the redemptive work of change. "For God, who said, *"Let light shine out of darkness,"* has shone in our hearts to give the light of the knowledge of the glory of God in the face of Jesus Christ." (**2 Cor. 4:6**). The word of promise was spoken to Rebekah during a period of uncertainty. This uncertainty stemmed from Jacob being the "**younger**," the second-born son, and not favored by Isaac. However, the word of promise served as a beacon of light pierced through this darkness, empowering the impending transformation. Rebekah held firm to this word of promise. Although Isaac favored Esau, God had chosen Jacob. Her struggles and labor, therefore, were not in vain in the Lord.

Treasure Your Promise

Jacob needed to transform from being the second son with limited inheritance and future prospects to become the bearer of God's purpose and destiny. He had to shift from inheriting the rights of a second son to claiming the birthright of the firstborn. Jacob also needed to evolve from being the son cherished only by his mother to becoming the son blessed by his father. This change was only possible because Rebekah continued to hold the word about Jacob in her heart.

Rebekah carried the treasure of the word of promise within her heart for decades. It is clear from the narrative that Rebekah shared this word with others, including Jacob. This promise is why Jacob negotiates for his birthright and swiftly agrees to participate in Rebekah's plan to secure Isaac's blessing. Rebekah's enduring faith in the word of promise ensured they were prepared when the critical moment arrived.

In the Gospels, Mary, the mother of Jesus, was entrusted with a profound word of promise that her son would save the world. From that humble setting in Bethlehem, she witnessed the guiding star at night. She held dear the shepherds' tales of the angelic host. Mary cherished the prophetic words spoken by Simeon and Anna about her newborn. She gratefully accepted the gifts from the Magi. She vividly remembered the anxious search for her young son when he lingered in the Temple, teaching the elders. Throughout her life, Mary treasured all these memories and insights, pondering them in her heart, reflecting on their significance and the role her son was destined to fulfill. *"His mother treasured up all these things in her heart."* (**Luke 2:51**). Then, decades later, Mary would draw from her treasure, approach her son at a wedding about a couple in need, and tell the servants, *"Do whatever he tells you."* (**John 2:5**).

Change unfolds in our lives when we embrace and carry the promises of God. The apostle Paul, aware of this transformative power, wrote a letter to his spiritual son, Timothy. Timothy, serving as the pastor of a church, was at a pivotal moment where change was essential. He needed to step fully into his destiny to evolve into a steadfast leader capable of guiding the early church into its next era. Paul wrote: *"This charge I entrust to you, Timothy, my child, in accordance with the prophecies previously made about you, that by them you may wage the good warfare."* (**1 Tim. 1:18**). Paul encouraged Timothy to utilize the "prophecies," the words of the promise he had received from the Lord, as a tool to combat any challenges that might impede his transformation into the leader God intended him to be. It was through clinging to these promises that Timothy was expected to evolve.

Similarly, when faced with daunting challenges within the church and critical opposition from others, Timothy was to recall the promises God had made to him. In a parallel situation, Jacob, confronted by an elder brother obstructing his path and a father indifferent to his role in God's design, was fortified by remembering the word given to Rebekah. These divine promises were anchors, empowering Timothy and Jacob to persevere and fulfill their God-ordained destinies.

Jacob did warfare with the word of promise. Change is always a fight, but the weapon of promise is *"divine power to destroy strongholds."* (**2 Cor. 10:4**).

Rebekah carried twins for nine months, but she carried a divine word for decades. She saw the fulfillment of the promise because she cherished that word in her heart and used it as a tool for spiritual warfare. Despite circumstance, history, tradition, and familial opposition all aligning against Jacob's selection, only God's declaration held significance for Rebekah. She placed her faith in the word of God over the word of man, guiding her actions and sustaining her through the challenges. *"Shall I bring to the point of birth and not cause to bring forth?"* says the Lord.

"Shall I, who cause to bring forth, shut the womb?" says your God. (**Isaiah 66:9**).

Rebekah had faith to believe the word of promise. We must have faith in the promises of God delivered to us in the Bible. But it takes more than faith to receive the promise. It also takes patience. The Scriptures say we should be *"imitators of those who through faith and patience inherit the promises."* (**Heb. 6:12**). Patience embodies the grace to wait and trust in God's timing, even when circumstances seem overwhelmingly adverse. Rebekah and Jacob held firm to their faith in God's promises, which gave them the patience to observe God's work unfolding in their lives. Through this divine intervention, God transformed Jacob, and through Jacob, He impacted the world.

Lessons for change

- Change only comes to those who are thirsty for change.
- God can change even the most barren situation or person.
- Prayer changes things, but it might first make you miserable.
- Change is a painful process
- Change is a battle of nature within us.
- The Promise of God is the power of God to change.
- The promises of God empower us to do warfare with those promises (**2 Cor. 10:3-5; Eph. 6:12,13**).
- We inherit the promise through faith and patience.

CHAPTER 2

Trade

As the boys matured, Esau became a skillful hunter and a man of the field, while Jacob was a quiet man who preferred to dwell in tents. Isaac had a particular fondness for Esau because he enjoyed the game that Esau caught. Conversely, Rebekah loved Jacob. On one occasion, while Jacob was preparing stew, Esau returned from the field, utterly exhausted. [30], Esau said to Jacob, "Let me eat some of that red stew, for I am exhausted!" **Therefore, his name was called Edom.** *Jacob said, "Sell me your birthright now." Esau said, "I am about to die; of what use is a birthright to me?" Jacob said, "Swear to me now." So, he swore to him and sold his birthright to Jacob. Then Jacob gave Esau bread and lentil stew, and he ate, drank, rose, and went his way. Thus, Esau despised his birthright.* **(Gen. 25:27 -34; Hebrews 12:14-17)**

Esau and Jacob were twins but not identical; they differed in many aspects. Esau, the firstborn, emerged reddish and hairy, which led to his name "Esau," meaning "red." Jacob, born immediately after, was holding Esau's heel as he came out, earning him the name "Jacob," which means "heel." From the outset, these brothers exhibited profound differences that extended well beyond their birth order, manifesting in their physical attributes, personalities, and destinies.

The Difference

Esau was described as a "skillful hunter, a man of the field," which reflects his character and temperament. Hunting can be an exhilarating sport and offers unique experiences; however, it carries significant risk and unpredictability as a way of life. Hunting offers no guarantees, unlike raising herds and flocks, which provide a consistent food supply and the potential for wealth accumulation. Hunters live from one hunt to the next, facing the constant risks of hunger or even death. In contrast to the pastoral lifestyle of his people, who relied on livestock for their livelihood, Esau opted for the precarious life of a hunter, choosing a path fraught with danger and the ever-present possibility of catastrophe.

Our text describes Jacob as a "quiet man, dwelling in tents," indicating that he was a rancher who managed herds and flocks rather than a hunter. This lifestyle choice reflects a preference for stability and lower risk than Esau's unpredictable and dangerous hunting. Jacob's approach was more about long-term planning and sustainability. He lived not by the day but by the seasons, which allowed him to grow and increase his wealth systematically.

The term "quiet," as used in this context, should not be interpreted as "soft" or "simple." Instead, it suggests that Jacob was contemplative or measured, focusing on a lifestyle that involved less immediate danger and more predictable, steady outcomes. The word "quiet" is the same Hebrew word used to describe Job as "a perfect" man (**Job 1:1,8,2:3**). It is the same word used in **Psalm 37:37**, "Mark the perfect man." The word means *"complete, peaceful, blameless."* Jacob was not simply a "Momma's boy" who stayed around the house while Esau was the "real man" out hunting in the field. Instead, Jacob was described as a "perfect" or upright man who took his relationship with God seriously. Both brothers were hunters in their own way—Esau hunted for game, while Jacob was hunting for God, seeking spiritual purpose and alignment with the divine promises in his life. Jacob focused not on worldly pursuits but on the deeper, more lasting pursuit of God's favor and blessing.

Although these brothers were different in many ways, the most significant difference lay in their approach to change. Both Esau and Jacob needed transformation, like all of us, to be formed by God. However, the crucial distinction between them is that Esau never changed. While Jacob would eventually become Israel, Esau remained the same. Esau enjoyed a blessed life, and his descendants became a nation for a time but did not walk with God. Today, the line of Esau has disappeared, but the spirit of Esau persists in those who resist change. They, like Esau, could have received everything, yet they chose to give it away.

The Birthright

The birthright referred to in this passage is the unique privilege of the firstborn son, as outlined in (**Deuteronomy 21:17**). When the father passed away, his estate would be divided among his sons, with the firstborn receiving a "double portion"—double what the other brothers inherited. The birthright made the firstborn the new head of the family after the father's death, granting him authority to lead and make decisions for the family.

As the firstborn, just a few seconds before his twin brother Jacob, Esau was destined to receive all these rights and privileges; he was positioned to enter into a covenant relationship with Yahweh and play a pivotal role in God's plan. In fact, God could have been known as **"The God of Abraham, Isaac, and Esau."** Esau was given an extraordinary gift and a profound opportunity. Yet, he traded it all away for a mere bowl of beans, forfeiting his birthright and place in God's legacy.

Hunger

God grants us the freedom to choose our way of life, but we are not free to choose the consequences. Esau also decides to be a hunter rather than a rancher. He accepts the risk of returning home empty-handed and hungry. Though he was often successful, bringing home a wild game that won his father's favor, Esau returned with neither food nor energy one day. And Jacob was ready.

Jacob had prepared a pot of lentil soup, a rich red bean stew, and fresh bread. When Esau arrived, he was so famished that in the Hebrew text, he emphatically repeated his request: *"Give me a gulp of that red stuff, that red stuff, for I am so exhausted."* Seizing the opportunity, Jacob offered a trade—Esau's birthright for the stew. In his moment of desperation, Esau agreed, trading away his birthright for a bowl of soup.

Trades

We always make trades to satisfy our physical, emotional, or spiritual hunger. Each day, we exchange our time, work, and resources for what we believe we need. However, we don't always make the right trades. The right trades bring lasting value and change to our lives. For example, an addict trades away time, money, energy, and relationships to feed their addiction—an unwise trade. On the other hand, a person who pursues education is trading time and money to improve their future, which is a good trade. The quality of our lives is shaped by the choices we make in these trades, either for good or bad.

Many people have long believed that Jacob tricked Esau in their famous exchange. However, there was no deception—just an open, fair trade. Esau traded to fill an empty belly; Jacob traded to fill an empty life. Esau was hungry in his flesh, while Jacob hungered in his spirit. Jacob did not deceive his brother; he simply made a wise trade. Jacob gained the birthright of Abraham and Isaac for a bowl of soup and a piece of bread. Esau thought it was a fair exchange, but Jacob was the one who made the better trade.

The text says: *"Esau despised his birthright."* That is a strong word, to **"despise"** something. It is the same word used to describe Jesus in **Isaiah 53:3**, *"he was despised and rejected..."*. It is essential to understand that the word here describes an action, not an emotion. Esau did not have an emotional feeling of despising his birthright. Instead, his disregard for it was revealed through his actions—a spiritual act. Esau didn't despise his birthright first and then trade it away; he despised it in the very act of selling it. In doing so, he assigned a price tag to something priceless: his covenant relationship with God. It may seem unthinkable that Esau would trade such immense wealth and spiritual inheritance for a simple bowl of beans, but people always do this. Whenever we trade the eternal promises of God for the temporary pleasures or comforts of this world, we despise our relationship with God, just as Esau did.

Esau was hungry for food, but Jacob was hungry for God. Jacob sought more than just the financial benefits of the birthright; he valued it because he longed to be a part of God's unfolding plan through Abraham and Isaac. While Esau prioritized satisfying his immediate physical hunger, Jacob sought to fulfill his divine destiny. Esau lived for instant gratification, lacking patience and any thought of a future with God. In contrast, Jacob desired the lasting value of an inheritance in God for himself and his descendants for generations to come.

Strategy

Esau was a skillful hunter, likely using intricate strategies to track and capture wild animals. The word translated as **"skillful"** here means **"intricate knowledge."** A hunter must understand his target—habits, responses, and diet—and develop a strategy accordingly. Similarly, Jacob was also hunting, but his target was Esau's birthright. Jacob wasn't just seeking to improve his material life but pursuing Abraham's spiritual inheritance.

Jacob didn't prepare the stew by accident; it was part of a calculated strategy. He knew his brother's nature and prepared a **"red"** stew for a **"red"** man. Jacob acted with faith and patience, understanding that Esau would return hungry and willing to bargain. However, he also employed a strategy based on his intimate knowledge of Esau. This shows that real change requires a plan and a clear strategy.

The saying *"If you fail to plan, you plan to fail"* holds true. Change doesn't happen overnight, but it begins with intentional first steps. Effective strategies are rooted in knowledge, goals, and principles. By diagnosing the issue you want to change and gaining an understanding of it, you can craft a solution, which then becomes your goal. Following biblical principles will guide you in achieving that goal and bringing about the desired change.

For example, one of the biblical principles in life is from the world of agriculture. It is the principle of sowing and reaping-*"Do not be deceived: God is not mocked, for whatever a man sows will he also reap."* (**Gal. 6:7**). Whatever you plant or allow to grow in your life will ultimately yield a harvest. If you desire a particular crop, you must first plant the seed. Nothing grows without intentional planting and diligent care over its development.

Esau never planted for spiritual growth; he didn't care about it. He lacked a strategy to change his life and ultimately reaped what he had sown. Esau harvested a bowl of beans but lost a life that could have been filled with divine purpose.

In contrast, Jacob intentionally developed a strategy for change. The issue was the birthright, and Jacob knew that Esau's appetite for food would outweigh his hunger for God. Recognizing that Esau would not always be successful in the hunt, Jacob "planted" the offer of hot soup and bread. In doing so, he reaped the harvest of his strategy. He secured the birthright, aligning himself with the divine purpose Esau had forfeited.

Do we have a strategy for change?

Esau in the New Testament

The writer of Hebrews discusses watching over your heart in a discussion about Esau. "*Looking diligently lest any man fail of the grace of God; lest any root of bitterness springing up trouble you, and thereby many be defiled; Lest there be any fornicator, or profane person, as Esau, who for one morsel of meat sold his birthright. For ye know how, when he would have inherited the blessing, he was rejected: for he found no place of repentance, though he sought it carefully with tears.*" (**Hebrews 12:15-17**).

The phrase "**looking diligently**" in this passage comes from the Greek word "**episkopos**," meaning "**to look over.**" This is the same word used in **1 Timothy 3:1** for "bishop." A bishop in the church is someone entrusted with the responsibility to "look over" the congregation, providing direction, guidance, and correction based on their observations. Similarly, we must become "bishops" over our hearts, taking responsibility for what we allow to flourish or wither within. This means carefully monitoring what we love how we love others and ensuring that we nurture what aligns with God's will while removing anything that hinders our spiritual growth.

The text speaks of **"a root of bitterness,"** which, like all roots, grows underground, hidden from view. To deal with a root, you must dig deep to find it and, even more profoundly, remove it. We cannot truly change the outward aspects of our lives without addressing the **"root issues"** buried in our hearts. Often, during a crisis, as when Esau believed he was starving, the hidden things in our hearts are revealed.

Esau never cultivated his heart to receive the things of God. While passionate about hunting wild game, he never pursued God with the same fervor. The Scripture describes Esau as a **"profane person,"** meaning he treated holy things as **"common."** Esau didn't value the divine inheritance God had given him, so he traded it away for something as ordinary as a meal. To "**despise your birthright**" doesn't require hatred for God but rather a failure to honor the holy privileges of grace, treating them as common and insignificant.

Esau **"failed"** the grace of God. He **"found no place of repentance"** because some decisions cannot be undone. Though God forgives us, we cannot always reverse the consequences of our actions. Esau could not regain what he traded away. Suppose we choose to disregard the privileges of grace and indulge the fleeting desires of the moment. In that case, we risk losing eternal rewards and our divine destiny.

The Lord will declare, *"Jacob have I loved, but Esau have I hated."* **(Romans 9: 13; Malachi 1:2,3)**. When we despise the birthright God has given us, we risk His displeasure. However, we are not bound to follow in Esau's footsteps. We can make the right trades and pursue our destiny and purpose in God. It starts with responsibility for our hearts and aligning our values with what is truly eternal. The choice is ours: to be like Jacob, who valued and honored the grace of God, or to be like Esau, who despised and rejected eternal riches for momentary satisfaction. Our decision determines whether we walk in God's favor or forfeit His blessings.

The Ultimate Trade

You can often discern what is in a person's heart by their trades and purchases. Jesus Himself made the ultimate trade for something He deeply values—us. He valued us so much that He willingly traded His life for ours. He took our place of judgment on the Cross and, in exchange, gave us His righteousness before God. This divine trade reflects His immeasurable love and the worth He places on each of us. *"For our sake, he made him to be sin who knew no sin, so that we might become the righteousness of God "* (**2 Cor. 5:21**). Jesus died our death so that we may experience His life. Everything we have in Jesus is because of the power of trade.

The Lord wants to make a trade with us. You give Him your heart. He gives you a new one. *"A new heart also will I give you, and a new spirit will I put within you: and I will take away the stony heart out of your flesh, and I will give you a heart of flesh."* (**Ezek. 36:26 2 Cor. 5:17**). He gives us a new heart so that we can have a new love and a new life. Jesus will change your heart so you can change your life.

Lessons for Change

- What are you hunting? What do you want to change in your life? You will have to make a trade. You must trade time and effort in one area for time and effort in another.

- What are you trading? What do you value? Esau only cared about today, not tomorrow. He cared about his belly, not his destiny. Esau felt he made a good trade because he valued the temporary and the carnal over the lasting and the spiritual. Esau chose the trade and, in the choosing, despised his birthright. Your choices determine your destiny and your values determine your choices.

- What is your strategy? Jacob made this stew on purpose. He knew the nature of his brother and made a **"red"** stew for a **"red"** man. He knew Esau would return home hungry and ready to bargain. Jacob exercised both faith and patience to inherit the promises. Still, he also employed a strategy based on the nature of his twin. Change will not happen until you develop a plan.

CHAPTER 3

The Salvation of Isaac

"...May God give you heaven's dew, the earth's fatness, and plenty of grain and wine. Let peoples serve you, and nations bow down to you. Be lord over your brothers and may your mother's sons bow down to you. Cursed be everyone who curses you and blessed be everyone who blesses you!" As soon as Isaac had finished blessing Jacob, and just as Jacob had barely left his father's presence, Esau returned from hunting. Unaware of what had just transpired, Esau prepared his meal and brought it to his father, eager to receive the blessing he believed was rightfully his. And he said to his father, "Let my father arise and eat of his son's game, that you may bless me." His father Isaac said to him, "Who are you?" He answered, "I am your son, your firstborn, Esau." Then Isaac trembled violently and said, "Who was it then that hunted game and brought it to me, and I ate it all before you came, and I have blessed him? Yes, and he shall be blessed." (**Gen. 27:28-33**).

The story of Jacob receiving his blessing is full of drama and suspense. **It would be best to read the entire story in the twenty-seventh chapter of Genesis before you read this chapter.** We witness the timing of God in Rebekah's swift action, driven by what she overheard. Rebekah cleverly counteracts Isaac's blindness by disguising Jacob in Esau's clothes. Isaac, fooled by the scent and texture of his eldest son, hungrily consumes the meal and unknowingly gives the full blessing intended for Esau to Jacob. When Esau, the skilled hunter, returns with his own meal, he arrives too late and finds that his plate is complete, but his blessing is gone. Jacob had already claimed it. In his fury, Esau plots to kill Jacob, forcing

Rebekah and Isaac to send Jacob away for his safety, thus beginning a new chapter in God's unfolding plan.

Isaac

The story begins with Isaac and his loss of vision. *"When Isaac was old, his eyes were dim so that he could not see..."*. Isaac's blindness is more than physical; it symbolizes his spiritual distance from God. This detachment is evident in his failure to spiritually guide Esau, particularly in not securing a godly wife. Esau took two wives from the Hittites, a people known for their idolatry, highlighting Isaac's neglect in ensuring that his son married within the covenant community. This spiritual blindness reflects Isaac's waning closeness to God and contributes to the unfolding tension within the family. (**Gen. 26:34**). We remember how Abraham went to great lengths to secure Rebekah as a bride for Isaac so that his son would not take a wife *"from the daughters of the Canaanites."* (**Gen. 24**). Isaac's failure to secure a proper bride for Esau, despite intending to bless him, reveals his disregard for the covenant. Esau had already traded his birthright for a bowl of porridge and married two women outside the covenant relationship, yet Isaac remained determined to bless him. Isaac knew that Esau would not be faithful to God, and he was aware that God had decreed the blessing should go to Jacob. However, Isaac ignored what he knew to be accurate and acted solely based on his feelings. In doing so, Isaac mirrored Esau's actions, willing to trade the sacred covenant of God for the fleeting satisfaction of a meal. This reveals Isaac's spiritual decline, as he chose temporal pleasure over divine purpose.

The follower of God is always someone who walks with God *"by faith and not by sight."* (**2 Cor. 5:7**). Isaac is blind but refuses to follow what he hears. Isaac says, *"The voice is Jacob's voice, but the hands are the hands of Esau"* (**Gen. 27:22**). Isaac hears the voice of Jacob but allows himself to be swayed by the feel of hairy skin, the smell of Esau's sweaty clothes, and the taste of a delicious meal in determining the future of the covenant. He chooses sensory confirmation over discernment, ignoring the voice of Jacob, just as he ignores the voice of God. Isaac's indifference to the covenant's fate is evident as he blesses Esau despite knowing it would undermine God's plan. Were it not for the decisive actions of Rebekah and Jacob, the covenant would have been jeopardized. In essence, they intervene to prevent Isaac from fulfilling his misguided, rebellious desires, ensuring the covenant's preservation.

After Isaac blesses Jacob, Esau enters with a prepared meal for his father. When Isaac discovers what happened, the text says, *"Then Isaac trembled very violently"* (**Gen. 27:33**). Isaac's reaction is fear and trembling, not anger. His trembling is a sign of repentance, not wrath. In that moment, Isaac recognizes the divine hand in what has transpired. He does not attempt to revoke the blessing given to Jacob, nor does he seek revenge or punishment. Instead, Isaac accepts what has happened, realizing that God's will has been fulfilled. Rather than resisting, Isaac listens to Rebekah's counsel. He sends Jacob away to find a bride worthy of God's covenant blessing. This marks a turning point for Isaac, as he realigns himself with God's plan rather than his desires. Isaac even gives Jacob another blessing (see **Gen. 28:2-4**). Isaac's trembling is clear evidence of his repentance. At that moment, he realized the truth—not only had he been tricked, but he was also saved from a grave error. Isaac knew that God had chosen Jacob, yet he had come dangerously close to disobeying the word of the Lord. His violent trembling reflects the weight of that realization—how close he came to forfeiting the covenant with God. Isaac's repentance is not just a response to being deceived but recognizing how God intervened to preserve the covenant despite his near rebellion.

Esau

Isaac repents his decision and acknowledges that God has chosen Jacob, demonstrating a change of heart. In contrast, Esau refuses to accept God's decision. He does not repent, nor does he change. Instead, Esau grows angry and bitter, unable to face the truth of his choices. In his frustration, Esau "re-writes" history, claiming that Jacob stole his birthright when he willingly gave it away for a bowl of porridge. Esau's inability to take responsibility for his actions reflects his rejection of the opportunity to change and align with God's plan. *"Now Esau hated Jacob because of the blessing with which his father had blessed him, and Esau said to himself, the days of mourning for my father are approaching; then I will kill my brother Jacob."* (**Gen. 27:41**). Isaac and Esau share the same experience. Still, their responses could not be more different. Isaac, recognizing that what has happened aligns with the will of God, repents and changes both his attitude and actions. He accepts God's plan and moves forward following it.

On the other hand, Esau only perceives the loss of his blessing. He directs his anger at Jacob, blaming him rather than reflecting on his choices. Esau is dangerously close to following "the way of Cain"—refusing to change and allowing his bitterness to grow to the point of contemplating murder against his brother.

This contrast reveals the critical difference between repentance and rebellion in response to God's will. (**1 John 3:12; Jude 11**).

The story of Esau is told again in the New Testament says, *"See to it that no one fails to obtain the grace of God; that no 'root of bitterness' springs up and causes trouble, and by it, many become defiled; that no one is sexually immoral or unholy like Esau, who sold his birthright for a single meal. For you know afterward, when he desired to inherit the blessing, he was rejected, for he found no chance to repent, though he sought it with tears."* (**Hebrews 12:15-17**)

The story of Esau serves as a powerful warning to us all. We face serious consequences when we live according to our feelings and desires rather than by grace and covenant purpose. Esau's life illustrates a point of no return—a moment when one can "*fail to obtain the grace of God.*" We must recognize that we do not have unlimited time to change our ways. The decisions we make today shape our future, and if we persist in disregarding God's grace, we risk missing the opportunity for transformation. Esau's story reminds us that the time for repentance and change is before it is too late. Repeatedly, the writer of Hebrews says, *"Today, if you hear his voice, do not harden your hearts as in the rebellion..."* (**Heb. 3:7,15,4:7**). This quote from **Psalm 95** refers to the failure of God's people to enter the Promised Land during the time of Moses (**Numbers 14**). Their disobedience resulted in a missed opportunity for repentance, and the entire generation perished in the wilderness (**1 Corinthians 10:1-13**). While God's love is infinite, our opportunities to respond to that love are not. There comes a time when the chance to avail ourselves of His grace and mercy ends, as it did for the Israelites who failed to trust and obey God. This serves as a sobering reminder that while God's love is boundless, our time to respond and walk in His purpose is limited.

Esau never changed. He lived his life and ultimately became a footnote of warning in the covenant history of God. It could have been Esau's legacy, with God revealing Himself as the God of Abraham, Isaac, and Esau. The twelve tribes could have descended from Esau, and from his lineage could have come Moses, David, and even Jesus. But that place was given to his twin brother, Jacob. Esau's tears could not secure his place in grace because remorse over one's actions is not the same as repentance and actual change. Change requires us to alter our actions, not just our emotions. We must start to change today, for we may not have tomorrow.

Rebekah and Jacob

When Isaac made his plan with Esau, *"Rebekah was listening."* (**Gen. 27:5**). Rebekah still carried the word the Lord had spoken to her: *"The older shall serve the younger."* (**Gen. 25:23**). Rebekah heard the voice of the Lord, she heard the voice of Isaac, and she tells Jacob, *"...obey my voice, and go..."* (**Gen. 27:13**). Rebekah joins Jacob and gives him the plan to receive his blessing. Rebekah carries the word and then carries out the word in her life. She is a *"doer of the word"* and not someone who **"hears only."** (**James 1:22**). Rebekah acts and leads Jacob to his blessing, saving Isaac and saving the covenant with God.

Many commentators criticize the actions of Rebekah and Jacob for their deception of Isaac and the falsehoods they employed. However, it is crucial to understand their actions within the cultural context of their time. Biblical culture significantly emphasizes honor and shame, and in that society, a wife or son would not dare to openly condemn a patriarch's actions, as it would bring dishonor to the individual and the family, leading to resistance against such condemnation.

Rather than dishonoring Isaac, Rebekah, and Jacob acted in a way that ultimately preserved his honor, helped him recognize his own sin, and ensured that the blessing was given to Jacob as God intended. Their actions can be seen as acts of faith, honor, and obedience to God, reflecting a deeper understanding of the dynamics of their culture. They navigated a complex situation, aligning their actions with God's plan while respecting the cultural values of their time.

Rebekah is a type of Christ in this story. Jacob was concerned that Isaac would discover he was not Esau and he would receive a curse instead of a blessing. Rebekah says, *"Let your curse be on me, my son..."* (**Gen. 27:13**). Rebekah is willing to obey God and take the curse for Jacob. Is this not what Jesus has done for us? The apostle Paul said: *"Christ redeemed us from the curse of the law by becoming a curse for us for it is written, 'Cursed is everyone who is hanged on a tree"- so that in Christ Jesus, the blessing of Abraham might come to the Gentiles, so that we might receive the promised Spirit through faith."* (**Gal. 3:13,14**).

Jesus obeyed God and took our curse upon Himself so that we could receive the promise of Abraham. Similarly, Rebekah obeyed God and was willing to bear the potential curse for her actions, ensuring Jacob would inherit that promise. Jesus did not die on the cross for His own sake; He did it for us. In contrast, Rebekah gained nothing for herself, only the risk of a curse. Yet, she acted for Jacob and to uphold the covenant of Abraham in the world.

Rebekah exemplifies the work of faith through selfless love, willing to suffer to obey God. While we can acknowledge that the actions of Rebekah and Jacob involved deception, it is worth noting that the Cross, too, can be seen as a paradox of sorts—a means of redemption that emerged from the depths of suffering and sacrifice. Both actions, though different in context, reveal profound truths about obedience, sacrifice, and the lengths to which one will go for the sake of God's promises. The Bible says Jesus was *"delivered up according to the definite plan and foreknowledge of God"* (**Acts 2:23**). The Bible says, *"We impart a secret and hidden wisdom of God, which God decreed before the ages for our glory. None of the rulers of this age understood this, for if they had, they would not have crucified the Lord of glory."* (**1 Cor. 2:7,8**). The Cross was indeed a twist of divine irony. The enemies of God believed they were eliminating Jesus. Still, they became the unwitting executioners of grace that redeemed the world. They thought His death marked the end when it was the beginning of a new covenant. If they had known that Jesus would rise from the dead, they would never have chosen to kill Him. In their misguided actions, they were tricked into bringing blessings to the world.

Similarly, in his disobedience and desire to bless Esau fully, Isaac had to be tricked into blessing the man God had chosen. Jacob donned Esau's clothes and used lambskins to mimic his brother's hairiness, leading Esau to approach Isaac and receive the blessing.

Yet, Jesus did far more than that. He took on our likeness and bore our sins and curses, offering Himself the ultimate sacrifice for our redemption. In doing so, He fulfilled the deepest purpose of God's plan, transforming what appeared to be defeat into the greatest victory for humanity. Jesus did not just **"put on"** humanity. He *"became flesh and dwelt among us."* Jesus became one of us, so we died when He died. When He rose from the dead, we rose from the dead. When He ascended to the throne of God, we ascended to the throne with Him. (**Rom. 6:3-11; Eph. 2:4-6**). And now, as we live as followers of Jesus, we are called to "put on the Lord Jesus Christ." (**Rom. 13:14**). Jacob approached Isaac clothed as Esau. We approach the throne of grace clothed with the righteousness of Christ. Jacob putting on Esau is a type of Christ and the believer.

The Way of Change

Our transformation is rooted in our relationship with Jesus. He took on our nature so we might be changed into His nature. While we will never become God, we can strive to become "like Him" in our character and how we live our lives. Becoming more Christlike is central to our faith and reflects His love and grace's profound impact on us. We are empowered to grow and reflect His qualities daily through our connection with Him. The Bible says, *"He has granted to us his precious and very great promises, that through them you may become partakers of the divine nature."* (**2 Pet. 1:4**). Paul uses the language of changing clothes when he exhorts us to *"put off your old self"* and *"put on your new self, created after the likeness of God in true righteousness and holiness."* (**Eph. 4:22-24**). Based on what Jesus did for us, we are empowered to make changes and decisions in our lives.

Real, lasting change is possible through Jesus, but we should never assume we are called to navigate this journey alone. When we follow Christ, we become part of His body, the church. The promises of God are granted to us collectively, not just to each individual alone. Just as the strength of holding a book comes from the connection of your hands to your wrists and arms, the power of God flows to us through our connection to the rest of the body—the church. (**Eph. 4:16**). We are called to grow and change as we unite in His name through worship and fellowship. Our power with God is directly linked to our connection with His people. When we come together in community, supporting and encouraging one another, we strengthen our relationship with God and enhance our ability to experience His presence and blessings. As Paul said, *"The eye cannot say to the hand, 'I have no need of you."* (**1 Cor. 12:21**). Jacob received the blessing of God through the actions of others. We need the family of God to fulfill the will of God for our lives.

Lessons of Change

- *"Faith apart from works is dead."* (**James 2:26**). Rebekah did not just "**hear**" the word; she developed a strategy for obedience and did the work of faith. Change will not just happen. Change only happens when you combine faith and work together. It is not enough to receive a promise or desire to change. It takes faith to step out and take action to change our lives.

- Not everybody is happy when you change. Esau was not happy that Jacob received his blessing. There will always be family and friends that resist change in your life because they think it will affect their status and place. Esau wanted a "**first place**" life with a "**second place**" effort. Esau thought that just because he was born, he should stay first without questioning faithfulness or purpose. Your success as you change will sometimes be seen as a threat to others. Jacob has to say "**goodbye**" to his past relationships to continue in his present blessing. Not every relationship can handle your change.

- Others must be involved. Rebekah and Jacob needed to cause Isaac to confront his sin. Sometimes, we are blind to our own need to change. We need a voice from another to lead us in a better direction. Moses needed the advice of Jethro (**Ex. 18**). David needed the voice of Nathan (**2 Sam. 12**). Peter needed the rebuke of Paul (**Gal. 2:11-14**). The Bible says, "Reprove a wise man, and he will love you." (**Prov. 9:8**). It is essential to be in a local church and have people in your life who can speak the truth in love (**Eph. 4:15**).

CHAPTER 4

Revelation

*Jacob left Beersheba and went toward Haran. He came to a particular place and stayed there that night because the sun had set. Taking one of the stones from the place, he put it under his head and lay down to sleep. He dreamed, and behold, a ladder was set up on the earth, with its top reaching heaven. And behold, the angels of God were ascending and descending on it! And behold, the Lord stood above it and said, "I am the Lord, the God of Abraham, your father and the God of Isaac. I will give the land on which you lie to you and your offspring. Your offspring shall be like the dust of the earth, and you shall spread abroad to the west and to the east and to the north and to the south, and in you and your offspring shall all the families of the earth be blessed. Behold, I am with you and will keep you wherever you go and bring you back to this land. I will not leave you until I have done what I promised you." Then Jacob awoke and said, "Surely the Lord is in this place, and I did not know it." And he was afraid and said, "How awesome is this place! This is none other than the house of God, and this is the gate of heaven." So early in the morning, Jacob took the stone he had put under his head, set it up for a pillar, and poured oil on top of it. He called the name of that place Bethel, but the city's name was Luz at first. Then Jacob made a vow, saying, "If God will be with me and will keep me in this way that I go, and will give me bread to eat and clothing to wear so that I come again to my father's house in peace, then the Lord shall be my God, and this stone, which I have set up for a pillar, shall be God's house. And of all that you give me, I will give a full tenth to you." (**Gen. 28:10-22**)*

Jacob, the second-born son with the right of the firstborn and the blessing of Isaac, heads to Haran to find a wife. Jacob has a responsibility to the covenant of Abraham to marry someone who follows the same God and is from the same family. He also leaves to give Esau time to accept Jacob's new status. Perhaps for the first time in his life, Jacob is truly alone. He sets out on a five-hundred-mile trip with nothing but the birthright and blessing of God.

Jacob has an experience with God. This is an essential element of change. Jacob has heard all the stories of Abraham, Sarah, Isaac, and Rebekah. But people do not change based on what others have experienced with God. We are changed by what we experience ourselves. Jacob was blessed by Isaac, but that is not enough. God gives Jacob a vision in this dream, a vision of the presence and promise of God. Through a dream, Jacob sees that his world is more than he ever realized, that the Lord his family served was real, and that this Lord is present and full of promise. This experience with God marks a new beginning in Jacob's life.

There are three dimensions to an experience with God: revelation, interpretation, and response. Jacob has a dream; he interprets the dream and then responds with a vow to the revelation he has received. We must be careful not to confuse these three dimensions as equally valid. The experience of God revealing Himself to Jacob is the most important element of this encounter. The response of Jacob is also essential. But we shall see that Jacob has a true revelation but misinterprets the event's significance. Jacob has a dream. He sees a **"ladder."** Some scholars suggest that what Jacob saw was not just a ladder but a stairway or a set of steps resembling a ramp or pyramid. Regardless of the exact nature of the structure, the ladder symbolizes the connection between heaven and earth. Jacob observed angels, messengers of God, ascending from earth to heaven and descending from heaven to earth. At the top of the ladder, he saw the Lord, who told him the promises made to Abraham and Isaac—promises of land, blessings on his descendants, and the assurance of His continued presence in Jacob's life.

Jacob was assured that the Lord would accompany him on his journey and bring him back to the land. What is remarkable about this dream is the absence of any words of correction or conditions. God promises Jacob His presence and grace without requiring anything in return. The promise is unconditional. Jacob is allowed to witness the heavenly host in action, the Lord at the top of the ladder, and to receive profound promises filled with grace and power without any demands for repentance or change.

The Bible says, "God's kindness is meant to lead you to repentance." (**Rom. 2:4**). It is the unconditional blessing that becomes the condition of the response of Jacob. It is the goodness and kindness of God that moves Jacob to make Yahweh his Lord.

When faced with the need to change, it's easy to feel overwhelmed and discouraged. The pursuit of change can be burdened by our past failures and pain. Jacob, embarking on a journey of hundreds of miles into the unknown, finds himself alone, carrying the weight of his failed relationships with his father and brother. Yet, he soon discovers that he is not alone, surrounded by an army of angels. The Lord of heaven and earth promises His abiding presence and faithful promises. Jacob is assured of a successful return before his journey begins. In our journeys of change, we have this same assurance and much more. We are accompanied by the presence of God, who supports and guides us through every challenge we face. We have more than a dream; we have *"the knowledge of the glory of God in the face of Jesus Christ."* (**2 Cor. 4:6**). We have the Lord at the top of Jacob's ladder with us, who *"was declared to be the Son of God in power according to the Spirit of holiness by his resurrection from the dead, Jesus Christ our Lord."* (**Rom. 1:4**). He will never leave us until our work of change is completed.

Jacob responds in worship by anointing the stone as his makeshift pillow and erecting it as a pillar. He renames the place "Bethel," meaning "the house of God." In this act of devotion, Jacob vows loyalty to the Lord and promises to give a tithe—ten percent of his wealth—to God. This mirrors Abraham's encounter with the king/priest Melchizedek, where Abraham also responded by giving a tithe. Similarly, when Jacob encounters the Lord in his dream, he may not have anything material to offer at that moment. Still, he commits to following in the worship of Abraham, recognizing the significance of his relationship with God.

The experience was real, and his response was genuine. Jacob's pledge of the tithe is a pledge of the heart, as Jesus said, *"Where your treasure is, there your heart will also be."* (**Mat. 6:21**). Jacob responds to the revelation but also misinterprets its significance. He believes he has stumbled upon a unique place—the house of God—without realizing that he is the special place. Jacob is the catalyst for the angelic activity in the area, not the location itself. Jacob embodies the presence and promise of God; it is within him that God's purpose is being fulfilled, rather than solely in Bethel.

The Lord never said that the place was special. Jacob did. The Lord never told Jacob to anoint a stone or to rename the place.

Jacob did that. Later, Jacob returned to this place at a critical time in his journey, *"and there he built an altar and called the place El-bethel because there God had revealed himself to him when he fled from his brother."* (**Gen. 35:7**). When Jacob returns years later, he is no longer honoring a place as much as the God who revealed Himself in that place, for the name "**El-Bethel**" means "*God of the house of God.*" The place was only special because the experience with God was special. Jacob is the sacred space, not Bethel.

Jesus told the disciple, Nathanael, *"Truly, truly I say to you, you will see heaven opened and the angels of God ascending and descending on the Son of Man."* (**John 1:21**). Jesus declares that He is the sacred space of God on earth, serving as the new Jacob—the one who connects heaven and earth. While Jesus fully understood His identity and purpose, Jacob had yet to recognize his significance in God's plan. He mistakenly believed Bethel was the sacred place rather than realizing he was the vessel of God's presence and promise.

The Story, We Tell Ourselves

The Bible is rich with stories because people are inherently full of stories. We live and die by the narratives we tell ourselves. Jacob has a dream, but he then interprets it through his own lens, believing that Bethel is the house of God and the center of divine activity when, in fact, he is the focus of God's purpose on earth. It takes years of walking with God and experiencing His goodness for Jacob to understand that he is the unique place of God's presence. Only after he is transformed into Israel can he rename Bethel to El-Bethel, signifying a deeper understanding of his identity.

One of the significant forces for change in our lives comes from altering the stories we tell ourselves. This is why God has given us the Bible—a collection of stories that resonate with our own. Life change occurs when we engage with these narratives, as they become part of our own stories. Through the Bible, we can rightly interpret the revelations God gives us. **2 Peter 1:4** states, *"He has granted us His precious and very great promises, so that through them you may become partakers of the divine nature."* God provides these stories and promises to help us interpret our experiences, leading to transformative change in our nature.

Jacob lived his entire life in the shadow of being second. He was the son not loved by his father, and his name, meaning **"heel,"** carried the connotation of being the one who grasps but never fully attains. He felt compelled to trick Isaac into believing he was Esau to receive his blessing. Because Isaac did not value Jacob, it's possible that Jacob struggled to value himself. Growing up in a community that viewed him as the second son—the "loser" rather than the "winner"—likely shaped his self-perception. This narrative may have influenced his understanding when he received the dream of the ladder and the Lord.

In Jacob's mind, the significance of the place felt more real than his own worth, leading him to believe that Bethel was unique because he could not yet accept his own value. This internal struggle between his identity and how others perceived him profoundly influenced his understanding of his experiences and his relationship with God.

We will never change or become what God has dreamed for us until we can articulate a true story about ourselves. Our transformation hinges on changing our narrative. We are not defined by what others have said or how they have treated us; we are defined by what God says we are. We are so valuable to the God of the universe that He gave His Son to suffer on the Cross for us. The God who appeared to Jacob has done even more for us in Jesus than He did for the grandson of Abraham. God has made us His house. Through Jesus, we become the temple of God (**1 Cor. 6:19-20**). We are Bethel because El-Bethel lives in us by His Spirit. God has changed our story because He has transformed us into His dwelling place and lives within us.

The revelation of what God has accomplished in Jesus Christ brings about our change. This revelation requires proper interpretation, highlighting the vital role of a local church. We need a community of faith—a church family that believes the Bible is the story of God and His people. Jacob had a revelation of God but missed the whole meaning because he was alone and lacked a supportive family for many years. We will change as our church family teaches us the story of God, reshaping the narrative we tell ourselves. Jesus said, *"You will know the truth, and the truth will set you free"* (**John 8:32**).

Response

Jacob responded to the revelation by performing a ritual. He set a stone upright as a pillar and anointed it with oil. Although God never instructed him to do this, it served as an act of worship and re-enactment, symbolizing that just as the pillar was aligned and anointed, Jacob himself was set apart for the work of God. This physical action represented a deeper spiritual reality.

Similarly, there are physical actions that God has commanded us to perform that symbolize spiritual truths and reenact what God has accomplished for us in Jesus. One of these actions is water baptism. God has given us baptism to illustrate what He has done for His people in the past, what He is doing in the present, and what He will do in the future. Through baptism, we publicly identify with Christ's death, burial, and resurrection, reaffirming our faith and commitment to Him.

- Water baptism looks back to when Noah was rescued alive through the flood (**1 Peter 3:20,21**) and when Israel was redeemed from bondage through the Red Sea (**1 Cor. 10:2**). The same God who rescued them has rescued and redeemed us.
- Water baptism tells us who we are in Christ: *"Do you not know that all of us who have been baptized into Christ Jesus have been baptized into his death? We were buried with him by baptism into death so that just as Christ was raised from the dead by the glory of the Father, we should walk in newness of life?"* (**Rom. 6:3,4**). We are united with Christ and experience the power of his resurrection now in **"in newness of life."**
- Water baptism tells us that the resurrection of Jesus is our resurrection promise as well: *"For if we have been united with him in a death like his, we shall certainly be united with him in a resurrection like his."* (**Rom. 6:5**). We shall rise from the dead like we rise from the water.

God never instructed Jacob to erect and anoint a stone pillar, but we are commanded to follow Jesus through water baptism (Matt. 28:19; Mark 16:16). Responding to the revelation of God in Christ through baptism connects us materially to the spiritual history of God and His people. The story of Jesus becomes our story, serving as our interpretation of His revelation and the foundation for change in our lives.

Jacob also responded to the revelation with a vow of faith, promising to pay a tithe to the Lord. At that moment, he had nothing but his clothes and his staff. In contrast, Isaac did not provide Jacob with any wealth to secure a bride, especially when compared to the ten "*camel-loads*" of wealth that Abraham sent with his servant to procure Rebekah (**Gen. 24:16**). Jacob's only possession was the revelation of God. However, empowered by this vision, he believed God would bless and enrich him in every area of his life. Jesus said, "*For where your treasure is, there your heart will also be*" (**Matt. 6:21**). Although Jacob could not give anything to the Lord at that time, he believed in his heart that God's promises were real and genuine, knowing he would return with something to offer.

Sometimes, like Jacob, we may feel surrounded by a lack of resources and think that will never change. Yet, when Jacob received this revelation of God, he became a wealthy man that day. He understood that his life was about to change and put his faith into action. We change from the inside out based on the revelations God gives us. Change is activated when we respond in faith to His promises. Jacob's vow that day marked the beginning of his journey of transformation and wealth creation. We must look beyond our current emptiness and, by faith, believe that God will supply our every need. We need to return our promise to God, trusting in His faithfulness.

Lessons for change

- The revelation of God becomes our foundation to change, but only to the extent we interpret the revelation of God correctly. Jesus said you first must know the truth before the truth can set you free. The truth that you do not know will never change you. That is why we, a local Bible-believing church, are vital to your change in Christ.

- A vast army of angelic beings surrounds us in our journey with God. The Bible says: *"They are ministering spirits sent out to serve for the sake of those who inherit salvation"* (**Heb. 1:14**). God has us surrounded by his army as much as we are surrounded by his love. We can face whatever comes our way.

- We must follow the Lord in obedience to His plan and His way. One way we follow Jesus is through water baptism. This public declaration of our loyalty and unity with Jesus empowers us with grace and the divine ability to continue our change journey. Our obedience brings us into alignment with his promises and purpose.

- Another way to follow God in our obedience is by giving. Jacob vowed to tithe based on the revelation he received at Bethel. We manifest with our treasure what is in our hearts. Tithing into a local church will change your life. God guarantees it (**Mal. 3:8-10**).

CHAPTER 5

"Behold, It was Leah...

"...Then Jacob told Laban, "Give me my wife that I may go into her, for my time is completed." So, Laban gathered all the people of the place and made a feast. In the evening, he took his daughter, Leah, and brought her to Jacob. **Laban also gave his female servant Zilpah to Leah to be her servant.** *When morning came, behold, it was Leah! Jacob asked Laban, "What have you done to me? Did I not serve you for Rachel? Why, then, have you deceived me?" Laban replied, "It is not our custom to give the younger before the firstborn. Complete the week of this one, and we will give you the other also in exchange for another seven years of service." Jacob agreed and completed the week. Then Laban gave him his daughter Rachel to be his wife.* **Laban also gave his female servant Bilhah to Rachel to be her servant.** *So Jacob went into Rachel also, and he loved Rachel more than Leah and served Laban for another seven years. When the Lord saw that Leah was hated, he opened her womb, but Rachel was barren. Leah conceived and bore a son, and she called him Reuben, saying, "Because the Lord has looked upon my affliction; for now my husband will love me." She conceived again, bore a son, and said, "Because the Lord has heard that I am hated, he has given me this son also." And she called his name Simeon. Again, she conceived and bore a son and said, "Now, this time, my husband will be attached to me because I have borne him three sons. Therefore, his name was Levi. And she conceived again and bore a son, and said, This time I will praise the Lord. Therefore, she called his name Judah. Then she ceased bearing."* **(Gen. 29:21-35)**

Change does not conclude with a divine encounter. While such an encounter can shift our minds and give us a new heart, it takes time and discipline for our character and circumstances to evolve. Jacob encounters God on his journey, which marks only the beginning of his transformation from Jacob to Israel. His life becomes much more complicated than the blessings and divine encounters suggest.

We might expect that the God who speaks to Jacob from the top of the ladder would remove every obstacle to his blessing. However, what Jacob experiences—and what we all encounter in our spiritual and character transformation—is that God does not deliver us from our problems; instead, He changes us through them. This process is integral to our growth and deepening relationship with Him.

In the **29th chapter of Genesis**, we see how the Lord guides Jacob to the right place at the right time to meet Rachel at the well. Jacob demonstrates his physical strength and emotional intensity when he moves a stone from the well—an effort that typically requires several men. Overwhelmed by the providence of God, Jacob kisses and cries over Rachel, instantly falling head over heels in love with her. He then works seven years for her father, Laban, to secure Rachel as his wife.

However, during the wedding, Jacob's bride is veiled. After the wedding feast which the Hebrew term in **Gen. 29:22** suggests involves **alcohol**, he believes he has wed Rachel. When morning comes, he discovers that *"behold, it was Leah"* (**Gen. 29:25**).

This must have been a shocking moment for Jacob. God had spoken to him about his destiny and appeared with glowing promises. He had been led directly to Rachel, and everything seemed to align with a divine plan. Yet he wakes up to find the wrong woman as his bride. What a mistake! This type of misfortune feels unwarranted for someone called by God and destined for greatness. How could God have allowed Jacob to fall into this trap without warning? And how does one recover from such a profound disappointment?

Unrealized Expectations

One of the most significant obstacles to spiritual growth and transformation is grappling with unrealized expectations. Jacob had envisioned working for seven years and then spending the rest of his life with Rachel. Instead, he finds himself with Leah and faces another seven years of labor. This outcome is far from the life Jacob had imagined. It raises questions about the presence and promises of God—this is not what he expected. This situation is a powerful illustration of unrealized expectations and the challenges when our hopes clash with reality.

As a pastor, we hear the cries of unrealized expectation all the time:

- "I did not expect married life to be like this."
- "I never imagined my child would end up in this situation."
- "I always expected my parents to stay together."
- "I thought this was the perfect job until I was fired."
- "I always believed everything would work out if you worked hard and did the right thing."

Many lives and relationships are thrown away or destroyed by unrealized expectations. We expect our lives and relationships to turn out a certain way, and when they do not, we react with outrage, bitterness, depression, and a strong desire to escape. We begin to doubt the goodness of God and the purpose of life when our imagined plans are crushed beyond repair. Some people become abusive to themselves and to others, taking out their frustration and anguish on those around them. Others run away in divorce or substance abuse because life has become something other than what they expected or planned.

God Uses Our Problems

Jacob did not plan on a **"Leah"** in his life or marriage. That morning was one of the most significant shocks of his life. It was not God's will for Jacob to eventually father over 12 children through four women who all lived in the same household. God's will is for one man to marry one woman (**Matthew 19:1-6**). Yet, this is the process God used to produce the twelve tribes of Israel.

God uses the problems in our lives to change us. The Lord does not cause our problems but uses them to fashion and form us into the vessel He desires. When we have our own *"Behold, it was Leah"* experiences in our lives, remember: *"God causes all things to work together for good to those who love God, to those who are called according to His purpose. For those whom He foreknew, He also predestined to become conformed to the image of His Son, so that He would be the firstborn among many brethren;"* (**Romans 8:28,29 NASB**).

God will use your problems for your good and His purposes. He can turn challenges into opportunities to manifest Christ in your life and conform you to His image. Every difficult situation and every mistake can still be used by God to bring about change and growth within us. No experience is wasted; they can serve as steppingstones on our transformation journey.

The Apostle Peter wrote: *"Beloved, think it not strange concerning the fiery trial, which is to try you, as though some strange thing happened unto you"* (**1 Peter 4:12**). The word **"try"** is translated from a Greek term that refers to the refining process of gold. Gold is rarely found in a pure state. In ancient times, it was heated until it became liquid, allowing impurities to rise to the surface to be scraped off. The goldsmith would repeat this process, refining the gold until he could see his reflection in the molten metal.

Similarly, God allows the heat of trials and tribulations to purify our hearts and character, burning away what needs to be removed until we reflect His image to the world. This refinement process is essential for our spiritual growth, as seen in scriptures like (**Proverbs 17:3, Isaiah 48:10, 54:16-17,** and **Revelation 3:18).**

Lessons for Jacob

Jacob had to take responsibility for obtaining a bride rather than having his father arrange it as Abraham did for Isaac. When Abraham sent his servant to find a bride for Isaac, he was equipped with camel loads of goods and gifts (**Gen. 24**). In contrast, Jacob left with only the clothes on his back, likely due to his strained relationship with Isaac after the deception regarding the blessing. Jacob learned that burning bridges in relationships can have unforeseen consequences.

He must have felt he was reaping what he had sown. Jacob deceived his father by posing as Esau, and now Laban had deceived him by presenting Leah as Rachel. This experience taught Jacob that how we treat others often reflects how we will be treated in return.

Another important lesson for Jacob was the need for prayer and discernment. He desires to marry Rachel for her beauty rather than her character, demonstrating a gullibility similar to Isaac's blindness when he is tricked by Laban. Jacob ultimately learned to consult the Lord before making significant decisions

(**Gen. 46:1-5**). After twenty years of service, Jacob knew how to navigate dealings with men like Laban, and he left the situation as a wealthy man.

The Lord disciplines those He loves and calls into service (**Deut. 8:5; Hebrews 12:5-9**). The same God who shares His glory with us also shares our suffering (**Romans 8:17**). When God calls someone to leadership, He often allows challenges to foster humility. It was not just the forty years in the palace that trained Moses but the forty years in the desert that transformed a murderer into a messiah. Likewise, it was not the act of killing Goliath that prepared David to be king, but the years he spent fleeing for his life from Saul that equipped him to rule. There is no *"reigning without training,"* and the manifestation of Jesus in the world often requires us to face our own "**Leah**" moments.

Our mistakes are not roadblocks to success; they are steppingstones and building blocks for our destiny. The Lord transforms our "**wrongs**" into His "rights." Do not let unrealized expectations derail your dreams. While your destiny may not unfold as you expect, it will be fulfilled as God has planned. God uses the "**Leah's**" in our lives to bring about transformation and growth. Embrace these challenges, for they are part of the journey toward fulfilling your purpose.

Leah

Jacob was not the only one whose life was changed forever that wedding night. Leah was compelled by her father to deceive a man into marrying her, becoming unwanted and unloved by her husband despite eventually bearing him six sons and a daughter. Throughout the night, Leah remained silent while Jacob called out Rachel's name, longing for her sister.

Leah believed she could earn Jacob's love. After giving birth to her first son, Reuben, she thought, "*Now my husband will love me.*" However, this was not the case. When her second son, Simeon, was born, she expressed her pain, stating that the birth was a gift from God "*because the Lord has heard that I was hated.*" By the time her third child arrived, Leah had resigned herself to a life without love, naming him Levi, which means **"joined,"** reflecting her desire for some form of connection. Yet, even after giving Jacob three sons, she still felt hated and disconnected from the man she shared her life and children with.

Then, a change came for Leah. With the birth of her fourth son, she named him Judah, proclaiming, "*This time I will praise the Lord.*" Leah realized she would never earn Jacob's love, but she recognized that there was Another who truly loved her. The Lord was her faithful husband, and He had blessed her abundantly with everything she had, including her four sons.

The name **"Judah"** means "*to lift your hands in praise*" and also "to lift your hands to let go." These actions embody a sacrifice of praise: surrendering to the Lord and releasing what we hold onto. Some believers struggle to lift their hands because they cannot let go of what they are grasping, unaware that these attachments can hinder a deeper relationship with God. Leah could praise the Lord and release her need for love from her husband. She chose not to let bitterness, resentment, or negative emotions take root in her heart; instead, she allowed them to go and embrace a life of praise to the Lord.

What Leah did not realize is that, despite her considerable emotional pain, she was vitally important to God's plan. Without Leah, there would never have been the tribe of Levi. This means there would be no Moses to deliver his people, no Aaron, and no priesthood to minister to the community. Even John the Baptist, who came from the tribe of Levi, would not exist without Leah's contribution.

Additionally, Leah was essential for the tribe of Judah to emerge. Without her, there would be no David to confront the giant, no Solomon to build the Temple, and no Jesus, the son of David and from the tribe of Judah. It was through Leah that God chose to bring Christ into the world.

Leah was neither forgotten nor forsaken. She may have been unaware of her significance, but ultimately, she won Jacob's heart. Jacob instructs Joseph and his sons on his deathbed that his bones should not rest in Egypt. His final wish was to be buried in the land promised to Abraham and Isaac.

"Then he commanded them and said to them, *"I am to be gathered to my people; bury me with my fathers in the cave that is in the field of Ephron the Hittite, in the cave that is in the field at Machpelah, to the east of Mamre, in the land of Canaan, which Abraham bought with the field from Ephron the Hittite to possess as a burying place. There, they buried Abraham and Sarah, his wife. There they buried Isaac and Rebekah, his wife, and I buried Leah—*" (Gen. 49:28-31).

Rachel was buried under a tree. It was to Leah that the place of honor was given. Leah would take her final resting place with the family of Abraham, with Jacob beside her. Leah was given the desire of her heart somewhere in her journey of praise.

Life does not always turn out as we planned. Life can be difficult, painful, and lonely. Some things happen and relationships that we can never change. But we can change. We can praise the Lord and let go of our plans to embrace God and

His plans. To those who belong to Christ, nothing happens to us that cannot be used to form Christ in us.

Lessons for change

- Unrealized expectations can be a tremendous problem in life. Jacob saw the ladder of God, saw angels, and heard the voice of God. Jacob had high expectations for his future. But things did not work out as he expected. We lose faith and trust in God when things do not work out as planned. We must understand that God's plan is not based on our expectations. It is based on His goodness. We need to trust God even when we cannot understand God.

- We need to trust God even when things are not all good. The promise to believers in (**Romans 8:28**)is not that all things that happen are good. It is that God works all things into good. Bad things happen to good people. People will often be disappointed and let us down. But God is for us, even when we do not understand.

- We need to learn how to worship. Leah came to her "**Judah**" moment, and so should we. God loves us even if no one else does. God hears our cries and knows our needs. He is worthy of praise, even when life does not go our way. *God births Christ into the world through us when we worship Him.*

CHAPTER 6

Finances

"As soon as Rachel had borne Joseph, Jacob told Laban, "Send me away, that I may go to my home and country. Give me my wives and children for whom I have served you, that I may go, for you know the service I have given you." (**Gen. 30**)

God desires to transform our lives, including our finances. One of the most recurring themes in the Bible is the relationship between finances and wealth creation. Moses stated, *"You shall remember the Lord your God, for it is He who gives you the power to get wealth..."* (**Deut. 8:18**). Missionaries who reach new people groups with the gospel often witness what is called the **"gospel lift,"** which refers to the increase in finances and overall quality of life among those who embrace the good news of Jesus. This sociological phenomenon clearly illustrates the biblical truth that following God can lead to financial growth.

Prosperity is a natural accompaniment to our life in Christ. The Bible emphasizes this in **3 John 2**, *"Beloved, I pray that in all respects you may prosper and be in good health, just as your soul prospers."* Jacob left home without any financial blessing from Isaac, but he carried the blessing of God in his life. Even when Jacob faced financial challenges due to Laban's trickery, which forced him into seven more years of servitude to repay a debt he never intended to incur, God continued to bless him. Jacob prospered in all his endeavors despite his circumstances, illustrating that divine blessing can prevail even in adversity.

Jacob was born into a wealthy family but found himself working off his debt to his wealthy uncle, Laban. Despite his background, Jacob was merely **"getting by,"** living at a sustainable financial level. For fourteen years, he toiled to pay off the debts associated with his bride price. Although he worked hard, his finances did not increase while his family continued to grow.

While some may become complacent, Jacob recognized that God had more significant plans for his life, and his expanding family needed more than just their daily provisions. After fourteen years of labor, Jacob sensed it was time for a change for Laban to support his family. He understood that he needed to pursue something beyond mere survival, seeking a way to fulfill his family's needs and God's purpose for his life. The decision to change Jacob's financial life occurs at Joseph's birth.

For fourteen years, Jacob's beloved Rachel struggled with infertility, while her sister Leah continuously bore son after son. Rachel's desperate plea was likely repeated many times during those long, barren years: *"Give me children or I die"* (**Gen. 30:1**). Although Rachel seemed to place her hope in Jacob, it was ultimately the Lord who heard her cry: *"God remembered Rachel, and God hearkened to her and opened her womb"* (**Gen. 30:22**). The birth of Joseph marked both a source of joy and a pivotal change in Jacob's life.

No longer content with a meager existence, Jacob sought to negotiate a new contract with Laban. Over the next six years, he experienced incredible and miraculous financial blessings, transforming his circumstances and setting the stage for his family's future prosperity.

The Turning Point

"As soon as Rachel had borne Joseph, Jacob told Laban, "Send me away, that I may go to my own home and country." (**Gen. 30:25**). Notice how the Bible connects these events together. It was the

birth of Joseph that ignited within Jacob the desire to prosper and succeed. Holding Joseph in his arms, Jacob felt reassured that God had not forgotten him; he was cradling the answer to his prayers. Joseph's birth was a powerful reminder and revelation of God's goodness and faithfulness to His promises. When God remembered Rachel, Jacob was reminded of God's presence and the birthright and blessing he had inherited from Abraham and Isaac.

You will never achieve your potential until you believe in it. Jacob had been beaten down and reduced to servitude under Laban for so long. With Rachel's barrenness, he became as blind as Isaac to the presence and promises of God. However, one answer to prayer transformed everything. Jacob began to see himself not as a servant struggling to survive but as a son of the covenant. The Bible tells us that God's goodness leads us to repentance (**Romans 2:4**). When Jacob experienced this goodness through Joseph's birth, it prompted him to "change his mind" about his hopes and future.

With the birth of Joseph, Jacob refused to let the pain of his past dictate the course of his future. He would no longer be defined by the barrenness of the last fourteen years of his life. Jacob believed that God had something better in store for him, not because he deserved it, but because God was faithful. God is good and keeps His promises, not only to Jacob but to every believer. His promise within us is more significant than any pain surrounding us. We can succeed in becoming whatever God has called us to be, and this world's **"Laban system"** cannot hold us back. Only God can define our identity and determine our destiny. Until we believe, we will never achieve.

Sometimes, we forget that God desires to bless and prosper us. We can become weary and beaten down by the troubles of life, losing sight of our calling and the success that is ours. We must remember that we are not defined by our circumstances or what others say about us. We are defined by what God has called us and promised us. We are not servants of a **"Laban"** world system; we are children of God and overcomers through Christ. We are promised to *"reign in life"* through Jesus Christ (**Rom. 5:17**).

Remember

The Lord has provided us a way to remember Him, strengthen our faith, and restore our identity. Participating in the practice of the Lord's Supper within the community of faith ignites hope and faith for believers. When we take the cup and the bread, we *"do this in remembrance"* of His body and blood shed for us (**Luke 22:19**). Remembering the price Jesus paid helps us grasp our value to God. As we remember Him, we also reaffirm our identity. We recognize that we are not slaves to sin or servants of oppressive powers or authorities. Instead, we remember that Jesus has made us "kings and priests," like Melchizedek, who also offered bread and wine to Jacob's grandfather. (**Gen. 14**). Eating the bread and drinking the cup signifies that what Jesus did for us is now within us. Because Jesus triumphed through the Cross, we can overcome any adversity or trial that comes our way, for *"greater is He that is in me than he that is in the world"* (**1 John**). We are not defined by our past or our circumstances; we are determined by the promises of God. By partaking in the bread and cup, we remember that Jesus not only died for us but also lives for and in us, empowering us with resurrection power.

Negotiation, Faithfulness, and Work

With his renewed faith, Jacob begins to negotiate with Laban. After fourteen years of hard work and faithfulness, Jacob's debt to Rachel and Leah has been fully repaid. He informs Laban that he is ready to leave (**Genesis 30:25-26**). This freedom from debt allows Jacob to negotiate from a position of strength. The Bible states, "*The rich rules over the poor, and the borrower is the lender's slave*" (**Prov. 22:7**).

While going into debt is often a necessary part of life in today's world, the Bible does not condemn being in debt; it simply speaks the truth about its implications. Debt can limit your freedom, as your debt influences your decisions. This is why Paul advises, "*Owe no man anything, except to love one another...*" (**Rom. 13:8**). Jacob incurred debt for a season. Still, once he cleared it, he began to build wealth, ensuring that he would not find himself in debt again. Jacob negotiates a deal with Laban. Jacob does not request new wages but submits his notice to Laban that he is ready to take his family and go home. Negotiation is about what you are dealing with and what you are dealing with. You can give your terms when you negotiate from a place of strength. Before, Laban held all the power and was able to swing a deal that caused Jacob to work for seven additional years. With newfound faith and strength, Jacob makes a deal that will change his life.

The strength of Jacob's negotiation stems from his history of divine favor and faithfulness. When Jacob expresses his intention to leave, Laban quickly offers to negotiate a new contract, recognizing that his own finances have improved because of Jacob's presence. Laban acknowledges, "*...the LORD hath blessed me for thy sake*" (**Gen. 30:27**).

Jacob begins his negotiations by recounting his years of dedicated service: *"You know how I have served you...how your flocks have grown..."* (**Gen. 30:29-30**). He does not base his negotiations on his covenant blessings or divine favor; instead, he stands on the solid foundation of years of faithful and fruitful service.

You are more likely to achieve your desired outcomes when you negotiate from a position of strength—free from debt and backed by a record of successful achievements. Jacob's faithful history of accomplishments empowers his negotiations, setting the stage for future prosperity.

We must cultivate the boldness to negotiate our terms in this world. A wise man once said, *"You are never paid what you are worth; you are only paid what you negotiate."* The Bible states, *"The wicked flee when no one pursues, but the righteous are as bold as a lion"* (**Prov. 28:1**). Jacob was emboldened to negotiate because of God's faithfulness in his life and his record of hard work and achievement. Being out of debt allowed Jacob to negotiate from a position of strength.

While we will explore the specifics of this negotiation in the next chapter, it's important to note that Jacob ultimately received what he desired. His confidence, rooted in his faith and past accomplishments, empowered him to pursue his sought blessings.

Prosperity

The prosperity message in the Bible encompasses not only faith but also faithfulness. If you desire to be full of faith, you must also be faithful. Jesus teaches us to exercise our faith through faithfulness, *"He that is faithful in that which is least is faithful also in much, and he that is unjust in the least is unjust also in much. If you have not been faithful in the unrighteous mammon, who will commit to your trust the true riches? And if you have not been faithful in another man's, who shall give you that which is your own?"* (**Luke 16:10-12**)

In this passage, Jesus highlights three areas where we can practice our faith and build a foundation of faithfulness essential for increasing and blessing our lives:

1. Little Things: Significant events may seem to lead to success, but how we handle daily occurrences defines us.

2. Money: If you are not faithful with money, why should God entrust you with more? If you cannot be faithful with a dime, why would He give you a dollar?

3. Another's Property: If you cannot be faithful to what belongs to someone else, you will never be trusted with your own property. If you cannot be trusted with the temporary riches of this life, why should God bless you with the true riches of His eternal kingdom?

These principles emphasize the importance of faithfulness in every aspect of our lives, serving as a foundation for more incredible blessings and responsibilities. Jacob exemplified faithfulness in all three areas. After finally parting ways with Laban and leaving for home, he said, *"These twenty years I have been with you. Your ewes and female goats have not miscarried, and I have not eaten the rams of your flocks. What was torn by wild beasts, I did not bring to you; I bore the loss of it myself. You required it from my hand, whether stolen by day or night. There I was: by day the heat consumed me, and the cold by night, and my sleep fled from my eyes"* (**Gen. 31:38-40**). Jacob demonstrated faithfulness in the "**little things**" of everyday life, as well as in managing money and Laban's property.

His faithfulness empowered Jacob to negotiate a better deal, allowing him to work not just for Laban but with Laban and his family. Jacob's success stemmed from his unwavering commitment. The change in his financial situation did not come easily or quickly; it resulted from years of hard work. His circumstances improved not in days or weeks but after enduring sacrifice, deprivation, and discomfort. There were no shortcuts to his success—only steadfast faithfulness.

Faithfulness will bring reward.

One of the most significant changes in Jacob's life is in his finances and wealth creation. Jacob arrived at Laban's house with nothing but the clothes on his back. Still, twenty years later, he left with a large family and substantial wealth in livestock and servants. This increase in his finances did not occur suddenly; it unfolded over many years.

The financial change resulted from the Lord's blessing and guidance through hard work and tough negotiations. Jacob managed to grow his personal fortune in a hostile environment filled with ruthless competitors and amidst personal turmoil within his family. His journey demonstrates that no matter your challenges or how dire your situation may seem, if you work diligently and exercise your faith, the Lord can bless and elevate you to levels you never thought possible.

Lessons for change

- Prosperity is a blessing that comes from a relationship with Jesus Christ. Our relationship with Jesus creates faithfulness in us because of God's faithfulness. This faithfulness makes us a valuable asset to any company or business we participate in because we bring our blessing to every endeavor.

- Do we need to look at our business and finances again? Jacob changed the terms of his business with Laban at the birth of Joseph. Is something happening in our lives that causes us to pivot to a more prosperous future? Does God have more for us to do and to receive?

- What are the obstacles stopping us from re-negotiating our circumstances? Are we fearful of change? Are we afraid to take a risk? Are we allowing our past failures to dictate our future success? Are we listening to other voices besides the Lord's and His promise to us? *Jacob was as bold as a lion. Are we?*

CHAPTER 7

Birthing and Beholding

"Name your wages, and I will give it," Laban said. Jacob replied, "You know how I have served you and how your livestock has fared with me. Before I came, you had little, and it has increased abundantly. The LORD has blessed you wherever I turned. But now, when shall I provide for my own household?" Laban asked, "What shall I give you?" Jacob said, "You shall not give me anything. If you do this for me, I will again pasture your flock and keep it: let me pass through all your flock today, removing every speckled and spotted sheep and every black lamb and the spotted and speckled among the goats. They shall be my wages. My honesty will answer for me later when you come to look into my wages with you. If found with me, everyone that is not speckled and spotted among the goats and black among the lambs shall be counted as stolen." Laban said, "Good! Let it be as you have said." But that day, Laban removed the male goats that were striped and spotted, all the female goats that were speckled and spotted, everyone that had white on it, and every black lamb, placing them in the care of his sons. He set a three-day journey distance between himself and Jacob, and Jacob pastured the rest of Laban's flock.

Then Jacob took fresh sticks of poplar, almond, and plane trees and peeled white streaks in them, exposing the white of the sticks. He set the peeled sticks in front of the flocks in the troughs—at the watering places where the flocks came to drink. Since they bred when they came to drink, the flocks bred before the sticks, producing striped, speckled, and spotted offspring. Jacob separated the lambs and directed the faces of the flocks toward the striped and black in Laban's flock. He kept his droves apart and did not mix them with Laban's flock. Whenever the stronger of the flock were breeding, Jacob would lay the sticks in the troughs before their eyes so they might breed among the sticks. He would not lay them there for the feebler of the flock; thus, the weaker would belong to Laban, and the stronger would be Jacob's.

As a result, Jacob increased significantly and had large flocks, along with female and male servants, camels, and donkeys. However, Jacob soon heard Laban's sons saying, "Jacob has taken all that was our father's, and from what was our father's, he has gained all this wealth." **(Genesis 30: 28-43)**

This story in the life of Jacob is not a lesson on how to change the color of livestock. It is a lesson on how to bring change to us. The process Jacob used to change his sheep and goats on the outside can bring change to us on the inside. This story is in the Bible for us to learn from Jacob the principles of change for our lives.

Change is Work

Laban asks, *"What can I give you?"* Jacob replies, *"You will not give me anything..."*. Our lives do not change simply by being given things; fundamental transformation occurs when we engage in the change process. Most lottery winners find themselves broke within five years because receiving a windfall does not equip them with the skills to manage their newfound wealth.

When God brought the Israelites to the Promised Land, He did not drive out the idolatrous nations all at once. Instead, He stated, *"Little by little I will drive them out from before you until you have increased and possess the land"* **(Ex. 23:30)**. The Bible also explains that part of the reason for this gradual removal was *"that the generations of the people of Israel might know war, to teach war* *to those who had not known it before*" (**Judges 3:2**). God did not simply hand them the Promised Land; He developed His people through the wilderness and their labor to prepare them to receive and prosper in their inheritance.

Similarly, Jacob became wealthy for the rest of his life because he worked hard and negotiated for his wealth, understanding that true success comes from effort and engagement in growth.

Change in life is hard work. The spiritual and emotional "muscles" you develop in the change process allow you to carry the change for the rest of your life. The method also allows you to teach the next generation your process so they can continue a legacy of change and increase. Laban did not give Jacob the gift of change. Jacob was allowed to work and bring change. This is how God works. He allows us to work toward change and develop the character and ability to keep the wealth created. God does not change us in every area of our lives automatically. He allows us to enter the change process to develop and grow to help others along the same path.

Starting at Zero

Jacob made a deal with Laban: he would continue to shepherd the flocks, and every sheep and goat that was speckled or spotted would be his wages. Laban quickly agreed to these terms but then had his sons remove all the spotted and speckled livestock from the herd (**Gen. 30:35**). This left Jacob with a flock entire of unspotted, single-color sheep, meaning he would only be paid if his sheep gave birth to spotted offspring.

Starting at zero, Jacob looked out over the flock and saw no spots or speckles of hope. He had nothing but the promise of God and the potential of another day. And that is all we need to begin changing our lives. We have the promise of the God who created everything from nothing and caused the barren to be fruitful and fill the earth.

Never let a lack in the physical realm deter you from believing in the unlimited potential of the spiritual realm. It does not matter what things look like; what matters is that there is always life and hope because God is our provider.

Dominant/Recessive

Laban agreed to Jacob's plan because he understood the principles of dominant and recessive traits. He knew that single-colored sheep were dominant and spotted or speckled animals were rare. By removing all the spotted and speckled livestock from the herd, Laban believed he could eliminate Jacob's ability to earn a wage, effectively ensuring that Jacob would work for him indefinitely.

What Laban failed to grasp was that God has the power to override genetic predisposition. With His creative power, God can transform what is recessive into something dominant and, conversely, make what is currently dominant become recessive. This illustrates that God's influence can surpass natural limitations and redefine our circumstances, bringing about unexpected change and abundance.

We all have aspects that dominate within us and those that are recessive. This is why the Apostle Paul expresses feelings like, *"that which I want to do I don't do, and that which I don't want to do I do"* (paraphrase of **Romans 7:15**). The flesh often seeks to dominate and seems to win. Many times, we may *"delight in the law of God after the inner man"* but then feel the pull of *"another law in my members ... bringing me into captivity"* (**Romans 7:18**).

It can feel as though the deck is stacked against us, making change seem futile.

The good news is that our genetic inheritance of sin and death is no longer dominant. *"For the law of the Spirit of life in Christ Jesus has made me free from the law of sin and death"* (**Romans 8:2**). God can take what is currently recessive in your life and make it dominant while also making what is dominant recede. Sinful habits can diminish, and holiness can take precedence. We have all sinned and fallen short of the glory of God, but we can all be transformed from glory to glory.

Jacob demonstrated this principle by placing the spotted sticks in front of the strongest sheep and lambs when he desired spotted offspring (**Gen. 30:41**). He focused on strength rather than weakness. In our own lives, we know what actions will make us stronger and what will weaken us. If we **"play to our strengths"** instead of our weaknesses, our strengths will grow.

The Bible advises, *"If you have been raised with Christ, seek the things above, where Christ is, seated at the right hand of God. Set your minds on things above, not on things on earth"* (**Col. 3:1-2**). We need to focus on the things of God that will strengthen us and refrain from dwelling on those that weaken us. We can cultivate resilience and move toward a more fulfilling life by prioritizing our spiritual growth and aligning our thoughts with God's truth.

Molding and Beholding

It is our destiny *"to be conformed to the image of His Son that He might be the firstborn among many brethren"* (**Romans 8:29**). God shapes us in much the same way Jacob changed his flocks. When we behold Jesus through the eyes of faith, we are transformed and become what we behold. This vital truth underscores the profound impact of worship. Paul addresses this principle of becoming what we behold in another letter:

"Since we have such hope, we are very bold, not like Moses, who would put a veil over his face so that the Israelites might not gaze at the outcome of what was being brought to an end. But their minds were hardened. To this day, when they read the old covenant, that veil remains unlifted because only through Christ is it taken away. Yes, to this day, a veil lies over their hearts whenever Moses is read. But when one turns to the Lord, the veil is removed. Now, the Lord is the Spirit; where the Spirit of the Lord is, there is freedom. And we all, with unveiled faces, beholding the glory of the Lord, are being transformed into the same image from one degree of glory to another. For this comes from the Lord who is the Spirit" (**2 Cor. 3:12-18**).

In Paul's second letter to the Corinthian church, we receive insight into our transformation when we **"behold"** the Lord in worship. In 2 Corinthians 3, Paul references how Moses spoke with the Lord **"face to face,"** resulting in his face shining with glory. To prevent the people from being alarmed by the radical change, Moses wore a veil over his face (**Ex. 33:11; 34:32-34**). He would don the veil among the people and remove it when in the presence of the Lord.

Paul explains that we, too, are changed because our relationship with God is **"face to face"** (**2 Cor. 4:6**). When we worship the Lord, we are transformed into the same image. By beholding the face of Jesus, we are renewed by the Spirit, reflecting His glory in our lives.

The word **"transformed"** is a translation of the Greek word **"metamorpho,"** from which we receive our word **"metamorphosis."** This word appears three times in the New Testament:

- **Mat 17:2**- "And he (Jesus) was transfigured (metamorpho) before them, and his face shone like the sun...
- **Romans 12:2**- "Do not be conformed to this world, but be transformed (metamorpho) by the renewal of your mind..."
- **2 Cor. 3:18**- "And we all, with unveiled face, beholding the glory of the Lord, are being transformed (metamorpho) into the same image..."

The word "**transformed**" means "**to change form**," much like how a caterpillar becomes a butterfly. When we behold the glory of the Lord, we are transformed by that experience. Just as the sheep gave birth to what they were looking at, change will be birthed in our lives as we focus on the Lord. An encounter in worship with Him will transform us; the more we experience His glory, the more we are changed. We are transformed "**from glory to glory.**"

Notice the passive tense in this text: "**being transformed.**" Change is not something we accomplish; it is done to us by the Spirit of God. The forming and transforming described here are not achieved through our direct actions but occur within us as we engage in something else. The flocks did nothing different to produce speckled offspring; they gave birth to what they beheld.

We are changed by what we look at and focus on in our hearts and minds. Change comes from grace, not from our own efforts. The fruit grows effortlessly from our relationship with the Lord. All we need to do is keep our eyes on Jesus.

Unveiled

Also, consider that Moses was changed by the glory of God because he entered His presence with his face **"unveiled."** He did not cover his face when he was with the Lord. Actual change and transformation occur only when we remove the veil from our faces. Sometimes, even as believers, we can cover our faces in a spiritual sense. We may feel guilt or shame because of our mistakes or sins, allowing something to come between us and the Lord. This can eclipse the glory and hinder the transforming power of God. When we do this, we are not changed because we are not worshipping **"face to face."** Only the **"unveiled face"** experiences change; the hidden parts of our lives remain untouched.

From the very beginning, humanity has been hiding from the presence of the Lord. After the fall, *"they sewed fig leaves together...and the man and his wife hid themselves from the presence of the Lord God"* (**Gen. 3:7-8**). The enemy works diligently to bring shame and condemnation upon us because, while he cannot hide us from God, we can hide ourselves. The enemy cannot stop God's glory from transforming us, but we can choose to do so ourselves.

We might go through the motions of worship while still concealing our true selves from the Lord. When we wear a veil to hide our faces from God and compartmentalize our lives, cutting off the light of His glory from every room in our hearts, we remain unchanged.

The writer of Hebrews says, *"...let us also lay aside every weight and sin which clings so closely and let us run with endurance the race that is set before us, looking to Jesus, the founder, and perfecter of our faith, who for the joy that was set before him endured the cross, despising the shame, and is seated at the right hand of the throne of God.*" (**Hebrews 12:1,2**). We must remove any obstruction, anything that blocks us from seeing and focusing on Jesus. This text exhorts us to lay aside both "**weight**" and "**sin.**" Shame and guilt become a weight, an obstruction that causes us to linger in darkness and hide from the light of God's presence. We must stop looking at our guilt and sin and start looking to the One who takes it all away. *"Behold the Lamb of God, who takes away the sin of the world."* (**John 1:29**). The bride stops wearing a veil after the wedding. We are the bride of Christ (**Rev. 19:7**). Time to take away our veil.

Look to Jesus

This story in the Bible is not merely a lesson in genetics; it is a lesson in the workings of the Spirit and how we undergo transformation. What Jacob did may not work in the natural realm, but it holds true in the spiritual. We become what we behold. The flocks gave birth to the image placed before them, and we are no different—we will produce what we focus on in our lives.

Jacob took sticks, stripping the bark to create streaks and spots of white, and placed these spotted and speckled sticks in front of the sheep and goats at their watering place. As they drank, they produced spotted and speckled offspring. Jacob carved an image and positioned it where it would be seen and reflected in the waters, and the animals gave birth to what they beheld.

This is what God has done in Jesus Christ. He transformed a piece of wood into an image that changes us. God took the Cross, placed Jesus upon it, and told us, *"Take up your cross and follow me.*" When we look at the Cross, we see the spots of blood and the streaks from the lashes that struck Him repeatedly. We confront the horror of our sin and the price Jesus paid to set us free. We witness forgiveness for our enemies and for ourselves. We recognize the payment of redemption and the promise of resurrection. And in that view, we are transformed.

Lessons for change

- We all start at zero. There is nothing good in us that God did not place there. But God takes our zero and turns us into a hero.

- We are changed by the glory of God to the extent we expose ourselves to His presence and grace. If we hide from God, we will not be changed. If we compartmentalize our lives, hiding portions of our hearts from God, those places will always be dark.

- We look to Jesus. When we see His face, we receive the grace and strength to remove our veils, stop hiding, and start worshipping. *And as we worship, we are changed from one degree of glory to another.*

CHAPTER 8

Breakout

"The Lord watch between me and thee..."

Change in our lives can sometimes be a fearful and daunting experience. Transitioning to a new job or moving to a different city often requires leaving the security of the familiar for uncharted territory. Many people even remain in abusive relationships because they have grown comfortable in their dysfunction, allowing fear and insecurity to prevent them from changing their situation. While the Lord can bless you in difficult circumstances, He may also call you to leave them behind.

In the story of Jacob, we learn how to change our lives by letting go of certain relationships. Jacob and Laban had a working relationship that lasted over twenty years. Still, when Jacob became more prosperous than Laban, their relationship soured. Laban grew jealous and resentful, feeling that Jacob's blessings came at his expense. Jacob overheard Laban's sons say, *"Jacob hath taken away all that was our father's"* (**Gen. 31:1**). Laban's attitude toward Jacob worsened; the more Jacob was blessed, the more resentment he faced from Laban and his sons.

Amid these circumstances, Jacob receives a command from the Lord: *"Return unto the land of thy fathers and to thy kindred..."* And with the command came the promise: *"And I will be with you"* (**Gen. 35:3**). Jacob might have been tempted to stay and work things out with Laban, but the promise of God's presence offered greater security and safety than anything Laban could provide. Additionally, the Lord spoke to Jacob through an angel in a dream, affirming that it was time to return to the land of his fathers (**Gen. 31:10-13**). Jacob then shared his dream with Rachel and Leah, and together, they agreed, saying, *"Whatever God hath said unto thee, do"* (**Gen. 31:16**).

How to Know It Is Time to Leave

Jacob recognized it was time to leave based on the change in his circumstances, the Lord's command, and his wives' consent. This is how we can discern when it's time to move on. Circumstances alone should never dictate the direction of a believer's life. Whether things are going exceptionally well or poorly doesn't hold significance until the Lord says, **"Go."** Even then, there should be some agreement with those in significant relationships with us to confirm our hearing from God.

The confirmation of agreement provides additional strength to obey God's command. While Rachel and Leah may not often see eye to eye in our story, they united in their agreement at this critical moment. Jacob could flee quickly and entirely because Rachel and Leah supported his decision. Their collective decision-making empowered Jacob to take decisive action in following God's directive.

A Clean Break

When the sun rises in the morning, it leaves no trace of darkness or night behind. It marks a new day, known as the **"break"** of dawn. To enter a new day of change, we must make a clean break with our past. Too many people desire a genuine **"breakthrough"** but are unwilling to **"break away."** Some toxic relationships cannot be healed; breaking away is essential. Shame and regret may be tied to your past, which needs to be released. There are habits and lifestyle choices that will hinder you from fulfilling your destiny. You will never experience your breakthrough until you break away.

Jacob fled from Laban without properly communicating his intentions (**Gen. 31:20**). He feared for his life and the safety of his family, believing Laban would prevent him from leaving with Rachel and Leah and their children (**Gen. 31:31**). Jacob made a hasty escape, but it was not a clean break. It wasn't until Laban chased him down and confronted each other that Jacob could genuinely break away from Laban completely. You cannot run away from your past without facing it.

Confrontation is not easy but essential for making a clean break. Though difficult, the conflict between Jacob and Laban was ultimately a blessing from God. Significantly, Laban pursued Jacob **"on the third day"** after his flight (**Gen. 31:22**). Jesus rose from the dead on the third day. Jacob's encounter marked the death of his former life, leading to the beginning of his resurrection. While Jacob may have felt apprehensive at the sight of Laban and his men, the Lord granted Jacob the gift of closure.

Complications with Confrontation

Jacob did not inform Laban of his departure because he feared for his life and his family's safety, so he snuck away. Laban only realized that Jacob had left three days later, and it took him seven more days to catch up. This led to a heated confrontation, especially because Rachel had secretly stolen her father's **"household gods"** (Gen. 31:19).

The reason Rachel took the idols is unclear, but that act complicated an already tricky situation. The breakup was messy, and this theft aggravated the tension. When we do wrong—even against someone who has wronged us—it will never bring us joy or peace. Rachel's actions gave Laban moral authority to accuse Jacob and search through all of his belongings. While Rachel cleverly avoided detection, her actions intensified the confrontation between Jacob and Laban.

We often leave relationships that cannot be repaired. When we do, we may carry unresolved emotions that lead to unwise actions. Making a clean break is not always feasible, but we should strive not to complicate confrontations with sinful behavior. Rachel's theft was a significant misstep, as some argue that she humiliated her father and his **"gods"** by sitting on them. Regardless of her motives, it was wrong and led to further complications. The consequences could have been severe if she had been caught, potentially hindering Jacob's obedience to God in returning home.

We must not allow our emotions to sabotage our future by seeking retaliation for past hurts. Sinning against someone simply because they sinned against us is never worth it.

The Blessing of Speaking the Truth

After Laban found nothing during his search, Jacob confronted him, detailing twenty years of grievances and abuse **(Gen. 31:38-42)**. Jacob's speech was filled with emotion, fury, and righteous indignation, as he had been honorable in his commitments. At this moment, he unloaded a detailed account of the wrongs done to him. While Jacob's words did not change Laban, it must have felt cathartic for him to finally stand up and confront the injustice he had endured for so long.

Many people never obtain the blessing Jacob received that day. Often, we are unable to confront those who have wronged us. The person who harmed us may have passed away, or facing them might be physically dangerous or too emotionally traumatic. While Jacob was able to express his hurt directly to Laban, we might not have that opportunity. However, we can still find release and closure by writing a letter or journaling about the abuse or sins against us. We may never share or send this letter, but we can release the burden through writing and no longer carry the weight of the past. The Lord will provide a way for you to find peace as you break away from your past.

Boundaries

Laban was unmoved and unchanged by Jacob's words. Since Jacob would never return to Laban's house, they erected a boundary stone to signify the break in their relationship. They gathered a heap of stones to testify to their new boundaries. Laban evidently had **"boundary issues,"** as his response to Jacob's complaints was not an apology but a declaration of illegitimate ownership: *"The daughters are my daughters, and the children are my children, and the flocks are my flocks, and all that you see is mine..."* (**Gen. 31:43**).

Laban claimed legal possession of everything Jacob considered his own. However, those daughters were no longer his; they were Jacob's wives, earned through fourteen years of labor. The children belonged to Jacob and his wives, not to Laban. Jacob acquired the cattle and wealth during six years of hard work. Laban was attempting to assert ownership over what rightfully belonged to Jacob. Therefore, it was essential for both Jacob and Laban to agree on boundaries before either could move forward in their lives.

You will never experience significant change without a clear understanding of proper boundaries. Righteousness and peace cannot be attained unless you maintain appropriate boundaries. The Bible says, *"Remove not the ancient landmark, which thy fathers have set"* (**Prov. 22:28**). There are boundaries that should not be crossed in relationships. Whenever a move is **"out of bounds,"** there will be penalties and unwelcome circumstances in your life.

An example of a relationship boundary is found in **Gen. 2:24:** "*Therefore shall a man leave his father and his mother, and shall cleave unto his wife: and they shall be one flesh.*" Before the fall of man, the Lord lays down a boundary. When a person enters marriage, their primary relationship is with their spouse, not their parents. This does not mean the relationship is over. Married people still love and honor their parents. It just means there are new boundary lines laid down by the covenant commitment that supersede the previous boundaries of parent and child. When a spouse is attached more to their parents than their spouse, there will be conflict and struggle in that home. We cannot move the **"ancient landmark"** without dire consequences.

When a married person has a sexual relationship outside his marriage, it is a boundary issue. When a child rebels against their parents, it is a boundary issue. When the government exceeds its authority by law, it becomes a boundary issue. There is no righteousness or peace without proper boundaries, and there is no change until you respect the boundaries God has placed in your life. When a football player steps out of bounds, it does not matter how well the play was executed. It is out of bounds. The play is rejected. It does not matter how **"right"** or **"good"** the play was executed when you are out of bounds. The play is still wrong, and no one ever wins if they keep ignoring the boundary lines. Our life with God is no different.

Jacob could not save the relationship with Laban, but he was able to change it. Jacob was able to confront Laban and was empowered to erect a new boundary in his life. We cannot permanently save relationships, but we can change them and allow that change to work in us. We must forgive those who abuse and hurt us, even when we may never trust them or have a relationship with them. We forgive and change our relationship. We erect new boundaries to proceed with our divine destiny, free from the bondage of our past. Like Jacob, we can wake up to a new day and a new reality of blessing in our lives. (For further help, investigate a series of books written on the subject from a Christian perspective by Dr. Henry Cloud and Dr. John Townsend).

The Power of Memorials

Jacob and Laban created a **"heap of stones"** to memorialize their mutual agreement to end their relationship. This memorial served to mark their decision in time and keep it in memory. The use of **"memorials"** is a recurring theme in the Bible. The Passover meal has been practiced by the Jewish people for over 5,000 years, and Christians have celebrated Communion for over 2,000 years. These observances help us remember the past: *"This do in remembrance of me"* (**Luke 22:19**).

There is a purpose behind our rituals. Our memory of the past enables us to live fully in the present and to hold hope for the future. Memorials remind us of significant moments, helping us reflect on God's faithfulness and the lessons learned, guiding us as we move forward. These practices anchor us, allowing us to draw strength from our experiences and foster a deeper connection with our faith and purpose.

The Bible is entire of memorials for remembrance:

- All the feasts and celebrations are re-enacted yearly (**Lev. 23**).
- The high priest wore stones on his shoulders and chest *"for remembrance"* (**Exodus 28**)
- Joshua had stones from crossing the Jordan set up as a memorial (**Joshua 4**)
- God sets *"watchmen"* among His people to keep the Lord in remembrance through prayer (**Isaiah 43:26,62:6**).
- God has a *"book of remembrance"* of those who fear the Lord (**Mal. 3:16**)

Memory and remembrance are clearly crucial to both us and God. Marking significant events, especially relationship changes, is vital in our transformation journey. Over time, memories can fade, and we might forget why we chose to walk away from a relationship. Jacob and Laban recognized the need to create a collective community memory of their break, establishing a memorial to mark the space and time of this pivotal event. It was essential for them to remember the valid and necessary reasons for ending their relationship.

When we leave a toxic or damaging relationship, we, too, should create a memorial. This might involve writing it down, recording it, or involving others affected by the break. We must not forget the reasons for our decision. Documenting our pain can help prevent us from repeating past mistakes. It can serve as a warning to others about similar relational traps.

There is a reason that remembrance is so significant in the Bible, and there is a purpose behind this encounter being recorded in Scripture. When we break away from our **"Laban's,"** we must ensure it is a clean break and remember our past. This is the only way to live blessedly in the present and maintain hope for the future. Remembering the past not only changes us but also shapes our future.

Lessons for change

- Sometimes, a relationship cannot be salvaged. The ties must stop if we will ever move forward with God.
- A relationship break is something that usually cannot be undone. We need to make sure it is God's will. We need agreement from other people in our relationship with us. We need the right circumstances.
- Personal safety and family security are always important issues. Be safe.
- A clean break is better than a messy break. Whenever it is possible, it is better to plan a confrontation and a time for resolution.
- *Make a way to remember when and why the relationship split.*

CHAPTER 9

Wrestling with Change

"And Jacob was left alone: and there he wrestled a man with him until the day's breaking."

We do not change for God; we change with God. The Lord actively works within us to form His divine character. We cannot become the person God desires without encountering the God who calls and shapes us. While there are habits we can change and goals we can achieve, there are aspects within us that only God can touch to bring about lasting transformation.

God intentionally brings us to a place where we must engage with Him. When the people of God left Egypt, the Lord brought them to a situation between Pharaoh and the Red Sea (**Ex. 13:17-18**). He had to get them stuck before He could save them. Often, He leads us to a place of desperation before granting us deliverance. God must often deliver us from ourselves before He can free us from our circumstances. What the Lord wants to give you and where He wants to send you cannot happen until He changes you.

Jacob is on the brink of returning to the land of promise, about to enter the birthright and blessing of divine destiny. However, the Lord will not allow Jacob to receive this destiny, as it is not for Jacob but for Israel. Therefore, God must transform Jacob into Israel. The Lord will never change your destiny without first changing you.

The Lord could have simply given Jacob everything at birth. Jacob could have been born before Esau and named Israel from the beginning. This would have automatically granted him the birthright and blessing, eliminating the need for deception or decades of exile. But the Lord had Jacob born to struggle because it is through the struggle that Jacob became Israel through wrestling with God and man.

We are not only born for destiny but also formed for destiny. Some muscles only develop through exercise and struggle. What God wants to give us cannot be carried with the muscles we are born with; it requires the strength that comes from overcoming challenges. Jacob was not born as Israel but transformed into Israel through wrestling with God. This process of struggle shaped him, allowing him to embrace his divine calling and fulfill his destiny.

The Man

Our text states, *"A man wrestled with him..."* As the night progresses and the blessings unfold, Jacob realizes he is not wrestling just a man or angel but God Himself. As the darkness lifts, Jacob proclaims, *"I have seen God face to face..."* (**Gen. 32:30**).

There are many mysteries in the Bible, and how God manifests as a man before the incarnation of Jesus is one of those enigmas. However, it appears from this text and others that God presents Himself in human form several times throughout the Old Testament. This highlights the profound ways God interacts with humanity, often in ways that transcend our understanding.

- Abraham- The text says, *"The Lord appeared to him..."* and then it says, *"Three men were standing before him..."* (**Gen.18:1,2**). These men share a meal prepared by Abraham and Sarah, and then one of the men is referred to as **"Lord"** and promises a son to Sarah and

Abraham. (**10-15**). The Lord seems to appear to Abraham as a man and two angels (**Gen. 18:23,24**).

- Jacob recounts a dream to Rachel and Leah. (**Gen. 31:10-13**). In that dream, Jacob says, '*The angel of God spoke to me...*" (**v.11**), and then Jacob says, *"He said...I am the God of Bethel where you anointed a pillar..."* (**v. 13**). In Jacob's dream, the angel of the Lord seems to be the same person as the God of Bethel.

- Joshua- The text says, *"When Joshua was by Jericho,... a man was standing before him with his sword drawn in his hand."* (**Joshua 5:13**). The man tells Joshua he is the commander of the Lord's army. Yet, Joshua bows his face in worship before this man; the man does not reject the worship. Twice in the book of Revelation, John bows down to an angel, and twice an angel rebukes him because worship only belongs to God (**Rev. 19:10; 22:8**). So, this commander of the Lord's army is more than an angel. He seems to be the Lord, who alone receives worship.

- The parents of Samson- When Samson's mother is visited by the Angel of the Lord, she says, *"A man of God came to me. He looked like an angel of God, very awesome."* (**Judges 13:6**). In this account, the angel of the Lord does not receive worship. Still, the angel ascended in the smoke and fire of the sacrifice and was not seen again. (**Judges 13:20**). Then Samson's parents declare, *"We have seen God."* (**Judges 13:22**).

So, when Jacob was alone and in the dark, a "**man**" wrestled with him, but he was more than a man. We discover it was God who jumped Jacob in the dark. Many times in the Bible, an angel, particularly the angel of the Lord, is the Lord Himself. This was a part of the biblical story of the Old Testament, and many have **"wrestled"** with this idea for millennia. It may seem strange, but God works in Jacob's life and our lives according to His way, not ours. (For more information, see *"The Angel of the Lord: A Biblical, Historical and Theological Study"* by Matt Foreman and Douglas Van Dorn. Waters of Creation Publishing, 2020).

Uninvited Blessing

He came without expectation or invitation. The Lord ambushed Jacob in the darkness of night. At first, Jacob may not have known who was attacking him. Often, we do not realize God is at work until we reflect on the experience later. Jacob could not see the face of his assailant and was reduced to feeling around in the dark, shielding himself from the shifting shadows. At some point in the struggle, Jacob recognized that he was not wrestling *"against flesh and blood"* alone but wrestling with God.

Some of the greatest blessings in our lives will come unexpectedly and uninvited. The Lord does not operate on our timetables nor wait for an invitation. When Moses encountered the burning bush, he had no idea his life would change forever. When Peter was released from prison, it was through divine intervention. Yet, when Peter arrived at the church praying for him, the door was shut in his face because they did not expect God to respond in that way (**Acts 12:14**). God blesses when and how He desires. It took Jacob a while to wrestle in the night with the unknown before he realized that his greatest blessing would be found in his greatest struggle.

Intimacy with the Lord is not always sweetness and light. It can also be painful and exhausting. There are times of joyful singing and times of intense wrestling. There are seasons when He gently whispers and moments when His voice reverberates within us for days. He always seeks to bless us, but it may feel like He is breaking us. As the Psalmist says, *"weeping may endure for a night, but joy cometh in the morning"* (**Ps. 30:5**). The Hebrew word for **"weeping"** here does not merely indicate a few stray tears; it refers to deep, long, hot tears that leave a mess on your face. We do not receive joy without experiencing weeping. Still, with God, that weeping will continually transform into joy, and He will change us in the process.

At Night

Jacob wrestled in the dark of night. God does some of His best work at night.

- The world was in darkness when God started His creative work. (**Gen. 1:2**).
- "a smoking furnace and a burning lamp" passed between the covenant pieces at night. (**Gen. 15: 17**).
- During the night, the people of God walked on dry land through the Red Sea. (**Ex. 14:20**).
- Peter and Paul were set free from prison during the night (**Acts 12, 16**).
- And during the night, Jesus rose from the dead, and the angels rolled away the stone.

We measure our days from sunrise to sunset, but God begins His day in the darkness. Every day in the creation narrative has the statement: *"And the evening and the morning..."* (**Gen. 1:5, 8,** etc). God has always worked the night shift.

In **Isaiah 50**, we have these verses: " *Who is among you that feareth the LORD, that obeyeth the voice of his servant, that walketh* *in darkness, and hath no light? Let him trust in the name of the LORD and stay upon his God. Behold, all ye that kindles a fire, that compass yourselves about with sparks: walk in the light of your fire and in the sparks that ye have kindled. This shall ye have of mine hand; ye shall lie down in sorrow."* (**Isa. 50:10,11**). These verses convey that times spent in darkness, when we feel devoid of light, do not indicate that we are lost or abandoned by God. Instead, these dark moments are often where our transformation occurs. God performs His creative and redemptive work in the dark, and during such times, we must, like Jacob, cling to and trust in the God we cannot see.

Before the era of digital cameras, we used film, taking the negative into a dark room for development. This process only works in darkness. God keeps us in the dark for a purpose: He wants to develop His image within us (**Romans 8:28-29**). If we were to turn on a light and dispel the darkness, it would disrupt the development process. Isaiah 50 tells us that when we *"kindle a fire"*—that is, try to bring light into our situation before our night is over—God allows us to live in our error. When we attempt to illuminate our struggles with theological reasoning or spiritual clichés, we often fail to develop into the image we are meant to embody. The Lord chose not to reveal Himself to Jacob in daylight; sometimes, He intentionally keeps us in the dark.

Remember that God is fully aware of you when you are in darkness, burdened by a problem. He is not holding you back; instead, He is shaping you into **"another vessel"** (**Jer. 18:3**). This experience may not align with your expectations or desires, but rest assured, you are not alone in the dark.

The New Day

At the breaking of dawn, God struck Jacob below the belt (**Gen. 32:25**). God doesn't always play fair because He isn't playing; He is transforming. He cannot bring our destiny into manifestation until He brings us into transformation. Jacob won the wrestling match not because he was a match for God but because he refused to let go of the Lord during those dark times. *"I will not let thee go, except thou bless me."* Many have missed the blessings of God because they let go of Him during the dark trials of their lives. When we feel overwhelmed and outmatched, that is the time to hold on, for our blessing is on the way.

Jacob was alone, yet he held on and kept wrestling. He was in the dark, but he refused to let go. Even when he was wounded, many would give up and follow their pain instead of their purpose. But Jacob did not release God, even when it was God who wounded him. No matter what, Jacob's response remained: *"I will not let You go until you bless me."*

We must emulate Jacob if we want to experience the same transformation. We need to declare to the Lord, "You can catch me off guard, you can confront me in the dark, you can wound me if you choose, but I will never let you go. You are my source of blessing. You are my power to change."

The New Walk

Jacob was touched in his hip, and with that touch, he was moved from a place of strength to a place of weakness, from independence to dependence. This transformation was necessary before God changed his name. God was not wrestling against Jacob but with him, guiding him to a position and attitude of surrender. While we must work with God, we cannot do the work of God on our own. Only God can truly change us.

We can hold on to Him in the dark and refuse to let go, but we must not deceive ourselves into thinking that our effort and strength bring about a new day of change. God could have shaken off Jacob's grip at any moment. However, Jacob needed to reach the end of his labors to enter God's rest. He had to die to his own strength before he could be resurrected in God's power. Jacob had to learn a new walk while receiving a new name.

The New Name

"Your name shall no longer be called Jacob, but Israel." The Lord changed his name, signifying his natural and destiny transformation. Just as God changed Abram to Abraham, He now transforms the **"heel"** and the **"deceiver"** into a *"prevailer with God"* and a **"prince of God."** As dawn breaks, a new man limps into a New Day, forever changed. Jacob leaves behind the empty tomb of his past. He stumbles forward into the light of resurrection power and a new identity.

Another son of Abraham wrestled through the night in a garden all alone. His disciples slept while He wrestled, and drops of blood mixed with tears streamed down His face. God does not play fair. Jesus died a death He did not deserve to give us a life we could never earn. The dawn of His resurrection empowers us to change and become the people God has called us to be. Our weeping may endure for a night, but joy and transformation will come in the morning. Because of Jesus, morning always comes and always wins. When we receive the power of the resurrection, God changes our name and grants us the morning star (**Rev. 2:17, 28**).

Lessons for change

- God wrestled with Jacob, not against him. So many times, we think God is against us when God loves us so much that nothing can separate us from His love (**Romans 8:28-39**). God wrestles with us to bring us to a place where He can touch and change us.

- Never stop holding onto the God who is holding you. No matter how dark the night, morning will always come. God works his best in the dark night of the soul. Do not confuse darkness and pain with abandonment. God is with you even if you do not sense or see Him.

- Our change comes from the work of God in our lives. Our job is to go to a place of dependence and surrender to receive the blessing of His resurrection power into our lives. Resurrection only works for those who are dead. **Romans 6:4:** *"We were buried with Him in baptism into death, so that, just as Christ was raised from the dead by the glory of the Father, we too might walk in the newness of life."* We change as we seek God, who then changes us. We must seek God first, then change will come (**Mat. 6:33**).

CHAPTER 10

Peace

"And Jacob lifted his eyes and looked and behold, Esau was coming and four hundred men with him..." (**Gen. 33:1**).

You cannot change your past, but you can change your future by making peace with it. Jacob ran from his past for twenty years, and perhaps that's why God touched him, causing a limp—so that Jacob could no longer run away from what he needed to face. Eventually, there comes a point in our transformation journey where God requires us to confront our past. We may need to forgive others, seek forgiveness ourselves, and make restitution when possible.

Just as a surgeon waits until a patient is strong enough to undergo an operation, the Lord may wait years until we have the strength to face our past. But like Jacob, God will ultimately lead us to a place where we must confront it.

You will never conquer your past until you confront it. Jacob had no choice, and neither do we. Sometimes, we have warnings and can form a plan; other times, confrontation catches us off guard in the middle of the night. Whether we can prepare or must wrestle unexpectedly, confrontation is never easy, primarily when we have caused pain or loss to others. It can be emotionally challenging to face our past, but we must trust that the Lord who forgives our past will be with us as we do so.

Face to Face

Before Jacob faced his past, he encountered God **"face to face."** His struggle with God gave him the victory and blessing to confront Esau. The Bible connects Jacob's wrestling with God to his later meeting with Esau. When the sun rose, Jacob named the place Peniel, saying, *"For I have seen God face to face, and yet my life has been delivered"* (**Gen. 32:30**). Later, when he meets Esau, Jacob says, *"For I have seen your face, which is like seeing the face of God, and you have accepted me"* (**Gen. 33:10**). Perhaps Jacob said this because he expected to die in either encounter but survived both. Wrestling with God empowered him to confront his brother and his past.

When God changed Jacob's name to Israel, He declared, *"For you have striven with God and with men and have prevailed"* (**Gen. 32:28**). God does not compartmentalize our lives into secular and spiritual; our relationship with Heaven always impacts our relationships on earth.

The crucifixion symbolizes our redemption in Christ, representing vertical and horizontal dimensions. This shape is how we are called to live as Christians. The Cross directs our lives upward toward God and outward toward others. Jesus taught us to pray *"and forgive us our debts, as we also have forgiven our debtors"* (**Mat. 6:12**). The forgiveness we receive must flow out to others. Neglecting our vertical or horizontal relationships diminishes our ability to carry the cross. However, when we accept Jesus' forgiveness and extend it to others, our lives become Cross-shaped, releasing the power of heaven on earth.

Jacob has looked into the face of God, and now he can look into the face of his brother Esau—the brother who wanted to kill him, the brother he impersonated to claim the blessing of God. There are no disguises or masks; it's about to get real.

Preparation for Confrontation

On the journey toward change, we must confront our past. Jacob does this by returning home and reuniting with his twin brother. How Jacob handles this confrontation offers valuable lessons for us. The Bible states, "*Now these things happened to them as an example, but they were written down for our instruction, on whom the ends of the ages have come*" (**1 Cor. 10:11**). We can view Jacob's experience as a guide for successfully navigating our confrontations with the past to change our future.

Jacob takes proactive steps by sending messengers to inform Esau of his return. When the messengers report that Esau is coming with 400 men, Jacob is *"greatly afraid and distressed"* (**Gen. 32:7**). The Hebrew words here convey the fear and confinement one feels in the face of impending danger, realizing there is no escape. The last time Jacob saw Esau, twenty years ago, his brother had threatened his life (**Gen. 27:41**). Rebekah had promised to send word when Esau's anger subsided, but that word never came. Now, Esau approaches with an army.

Jacob responds in several ways. He acts strategically, dividing his livestock into two groups, so if Esau attacks one, the other might escape (**Gen. 32:8**). He prays to the Lord for deliverance and protection from Esau's anger (**Gen. 32:9-12**). He acts socially by sending generous gifts of livestock in three waves to Esau (**Gen. 32:13-20**). Finally, he acts selfishly by placing his family between himself and Esau's approaching army (**Gen. 32:21-22**). Then God intervenes, wrestling with Jacob at night and changing him with a single touch (**Gen. 32:24-30**).

Jacob emerges with a limp but no longer as a coward. He stops placing his family between himself and Esau, instead grouping them behind him, and limps forward to face Esau alone (**Gen. 33:1-2**). The time of reckoning has come.

As Jacob sees his brother approaching with an army, uncertainty fills him. He doesn't know if his peace offerings will be welcomed or met with anger; he fears for his life. So, he bows low to the ground seven times, demonstrating respect and a desire for peace. Surprisingly, Esau runs toward him. Jacob braces himself for the worst, but then he sees the tears on Esau's face. *"And Esau ran to meet him, and embraced him, and fell on his neck, and kissed him: and they wept"* (**Gen. 33:4**). This warm reception was something Jacob never anticipated.

Dealing with Your Past

What can we learn from this episode about Jacob's life?

First, when confronting someone from your past, ensure you are safe and protected. Jacob divided his resources into two before facing Esau so he would still have a way to live in case of an attack (**Gen. 32:8**). You must take care of yourself if you're going to care for others. Just as airplane stewards advise that in an emergency, you should place the oxygen mask on yourself before assisting someone else, you must ensure your safety first. If you stop breathing, you can't help others catch their breath. Similarly, you can't bring healing unless you are safe from attack. Never confront the unknown without knowing you are secure.

Secondly, a generous gift can significantly aid in building peace. Some commentators argue that Jacob's gifts to Esau were unnecessary since Esau welcomed him back with open arms. While that may be true, offering something in the name of peace is never wrong. Of the five types of offerings in the Bible, two are the "**peace offering**" (**Lev. 3**) and the "**trespass offering**" (**Lev. 5**).

Jacob couldn't give back the blessing. Still, he could share some of its fruits with Esau. Importantly, Esau did not bring a gift to Jacob and did not bow down to him. He recognized himself as the offended party, and Jacob's generous gifts signaled his respect and desire for reconciliation. Perhaps those gifts played a role in Esau's willingness to forgive so easily.

Thirdly, there's a crucial difference between forgiveness and trust. When Esau invited Jacob to return home, Jacob made an excuse to go alone (**Gen. 33:12-14**). When Esau offered to leave some men with Jacob for protection, Jacob politely declined (**Gen. 33:15**). While Jacob expressed hope to see Esau again, he traveled in a different direction once Esau left (Esau went south while Jacob went west, **Gen. 33:16-17**). Jacob understood that maintaining peace with Esau required keeping some distance. He had been transformed into Israel, but Esau was still Esau. Sometimes, you must say, *"I love you, but I do not trust you yet."*

You and Your Past

Someday, your past will come running toward you. You cannot hide, and you cannot run away. It will catch up with you, forcing you to embrace what you have done and the people you have harmed. You can protect, pray, and try to purchase your way out of your past, but you cannot escape the confrontation.

Jacob had nothing to fear from Esau, and we have nothing to fear from our past. Our God is eternal (**Isaiah 57:15**). The past and the future are identical to Him. The God who has secured our future also has His hand upon our past. Jacob gave gifts to appease Esau, but God gave His Son to handle your past. There is no need to fear. Whatever you face in this life, God is with you. Whatever we encounter after our time, God is for us (**Romans**

8:31-32). Only those who have not made peace with God through Christ have any fear about their past or their future.

When Jacob finally confronted Esau, he said, *"I see your face as one sees the face of God, and you have received me favorably"* (**Gen. 33:10, NASB**). Looking back at your past, you will not see your mistakes or sins. Because of His grace, you will see His face. Do not fear your past. Make peace with your past. That is the only way to change your future. And there is a promise to those who make peace: *"Blessed are the peacemakers, for they shall be called sons of God"* (**Mat. 5:9**).

Lessons for change

- Jacob used strategy in this confrontation, and so should we. When we deal with people, Jesus says, "Be wise as serpents and innocent as doves" (**Mat. 10:16**). You never know how people will act and how things will transpire once the confrontation begins. Choose a safe space. You may need people you can trust to be near you. Consider whether it should be in a public or private place. Have an exit strategy.

- Have a goal in your confrontation. What is it you want to accomplish? If you are wanting an apology, you may never get it. Do you want closure? What would that look like? Unless you have a clear goal and believe a confrontation can bring you that goal, consider that you may not be ready or this may not be the right time.

- Go to God before you go to them. Jacob wrestled with God all night. There needs to be a severe encounter with God before you seek to encounter your past.

God forgives us, but people may not. Are you ready if you confront and do not achieve your goal? What if that person does not apologize? What if you never receive closure from your past? Can you still walk in love and forgive those who have hurt you and will do it again? We need a touch from God to walk correctly in our relationships and deal with confrontation.

- Attitude determines Altitude. Jacob came in, bowing low. He sent gifts. He was doing everything he could to make peace and communicate an attitude of love and service. We have no power over our past. We cannot change it. But we have power over our attitude. We can change it. Jacob approached Esau with peace and appeasement, and it worked. We need to check ourselves before we wreck ourselves.

- Reconciliation does not always mean Restoration. Jacob confronted Esau and brought reconciliation to their relationship. But he still did not trust him. They do not join forces. They do not have family vacations together. They meet again at the burial of Isaac (**Gen. 35:29**) but are never mentioned together again. Sometimes, the purpose of confrontation is simply reconciliation, not restoration. If our goal of confrontation is restoration, sometimes we have to settle with reconciliation. The relationship can change, but the other person may not have changed. We need to know we can love them, but we do not need to trust them. Without trust, you can make peace but not make a life with them.

CHAPTER 11

Going Backwards

"God said to Jacob, *"Arise, go up to Bethel and dwell there. Make an altar there to the God who appeared when you fled from your brother Esau."* So Jacob said to his household and everyone with him, *"Put away the foreign gods that are among you and purify yourselves and change your garments."* (**Gen. 35:1,2**).

Transformation is continually allowing God to form you into His image. Lasting change results from a sustained and obedient focus on the God who has called and changed you. Too many believers have had rich and unique encounters with God that changed their lives. Yet, they stop growing and becoming, thinking they have arrived when, in fact, they are just beginning. No one is immune to sliding back into negative patterns and worldly lifestyles—not you, me, and Jacob.

When Jacob left his encounter with Esau, he "built himself a house and made booths for his livestock" (Gen. 33:17). He then went to a city called Shechem, where he "pitched his tent before the city" (33:18). Jacob also bought a parcel of land from the king of the city (33:19) and erected an altar called "El-Elohe-Israel," meaning "The Mighty God of Israel" (33:20). While these actions seem like excellent and regular activities for Jacob, the problem is that God never instructed him to do any of them.

Jacob inherited the blessing of Abraham, a pilgrim, a seeker of God, not a settler in the land. The blessing Jacob worked so hard to receive was not meant for building a house and settling down; it was the blessing of Abraham, who lived in tents all his life. Abraham never bought any land except the cave of Machpelah to bury his wife, Sarah (Gen. 23:9). He lived in a tent because he was not looking to settle down and become like the other nations. As it says in **Hebrews 11**, *"By faith he sojourned in the land of promise, as in a strange country, dwelling in tabernacles with Isaac and Jacob, the heirs with him of the same promise: For he looked for a city which hath foundations, whose builder and maker is God."* (**Hebrews 11:9.10**). Jacob no longer wanted to live as a pilgrim in the blessing of Abraham. Jacob wanted to live in the shadow of the city.

Jacob pitched his tent and *"camped before the city"* (**Gen. 33:18**). In Genesis, cities often symbolize disobedience, oppression, and sin. Cain, who murdered his brother, was told by God to wander the earth as a fugitive for his crime (**Gen. 4:12**). Instead, Cain built the first city in the Bible (**Gen. 4:17**). The descendants of Cain and their cities were eventually wiped out by the flood. After the flood, people declared, *"Let us build us a city and a tower, whose top may reach unto heaven; and let us make us a name, lest we be scattered abroad upon the face of the whole earth"* (**Gen. 11:4**). In response, God confused their language and understanding for attempting to build the Tower of Babel, leading to the notion that cities have often been places of confusion and misunderstanding.

Living toward a city has historically proven unwise for those called by God in Genesis. When Abraham set out to follow God, his nephew Lot joined him. However, Lot eventually chose to dwell in the cities, pitching his tent toward Sodom (**Gen. 13:12**). What began as a decision to move closer to a town led Lot to live within Sodom and *"sit in the gate"* (**Gen. 19:1**). Lot mistakenly believed he was advancing in life while actually moving away from God. Ultimately, he lost his wife and his family and even committed incest with his daughters—all because he chose to *"pitch his tent toward Sodom."* Similarly, all the misfortunes that befell Jacob and his family stemmed from his choice to "pitch his tent toward the city."

By purchasing a parcel of land and camping *"before"* the city of Shechem, Jacob established a relationship with that city. The terms *"towards"* and *"before"* indicate a personal connection. Jacob wasn't merely securing a permanent place to live but forming a lasting relationship with the city. Tired of walking by faith, he sought a place of his own. Although he didn't move directly into the town like Lot, he positioned himself to be influenced by it. Jacob did not seek the Lord's will regarding this purchase; he acted according to his desires rather than God's guidance.

Jacob then built an altar to the Lord, but it was worship without obedience and ritual without revelation (**1 Sam. 15:22-23; Ps. 51:16-17**). Unlike Abraham and Isaac, who built altars based on genuine revelation and relationship, Jacob constructed an altar to get God to bless his chaotic situation. Sometimes, we may do the right thing for the wrong reason. While God does not condemn the action, Jacob's altar and worship did not bring about the blessing or transformation he sought for himself or his family. It was a ritualistic act—an idea that felt good but lacked divine inspiration.

Focusing on the city life around him led Jacob's daughter, Dinah, to *"go out to see the women of the land"* (**Gen. 34:1**). She became captivated by the worldliness of the city. She was ensnared in a lifestyle that thrived there. As a result, Jacob lost the direction and purpose of his life, and Dinah tragically lost her virginity through rape. Her brothers, Simeon and Levi, devised a plan with the rulers of Shechem, convincing all the males in the city to undergo circumcision to become like the followers of Abraham. In their moment of vulnerability, Simeon and Levi take revenge for their sister by killing all the adult males in the city. Jacob and his family fled in fear of retaliation from neighboring cities.

Though Jacob would eventually return to the path of the Lord and retain his birthright and blessing, the consequences of his actions would linger.

The Way of Retreat

Every believer is called to be a king and a priest (**Ex. 19:6; 1 Peter 2:9; Rev. 1:6**). This calling includes exercising authority and focusing on the Lord through worship and obedience. When we fail to embody this role, neglecting our jurisdiction and concentrating on anything other than God, we inevitably drift away from our purpose and His Presence.

Jacob focused on the city of man instead of his pilgrimage toward the city of God (**Hebrews 11:9-10**). He did not take responsibility for keeping Dinah away from the city and failed to act when she was raped (**Gen. 34:5**). Instead of confronting the situation himself, he waited for his sons to address it. It was Simeon and Levi who misused the rite of circumcision, commanded by God to Abraham and his descendants, as a weapon of war. By not stepping into his role as king and priest at home, Jacob allowed the situation to spiral into death and destruction.

The Way Back

God speaks a word to him in the murky darkness of Jacob's confusion. *"Arise, go up to Bethel, and dwell there: and make there an altar unto God that appeared unto thee when thou fleddest from the face of Esau, thy brother."* (**Gen. 35:1**). This is the grace of God. God speaks a word into our life. We have made mistakes and grown away from Him, but He does not go away from us. The Bible says, *"If we are faithless, he remains faithful, for he cannot deny Himself."* (**2 Tim. 2:13**). Jacob tried to form a new life in his own power and failed. But God has not given up on Jacob and calls him back. Jacob must go back to Bethel, where he saw the vision of God and was renewed in his mind. He must return to Bethel, where he started, to start something new.

This is an essential truth in the journey of change. Sometimes, we get lost on the way. We lose our focus. We fail to keep growing, backslide into comfort, and lose the fire of our purpose and calling. Sometimes, we slide into sin and lose sight of our identity and calling in God. The truth is that God does not throw us away. He will not always rescue us from the consequences of our actions, but He will never leave or forsake us. (**Heb. 13:5**). God asks us to re-connect instead of throwing us away. God tells Jacob to go back to Bethel to reconnect with the God again. Sometimes, we must go backward in our journey to go forward. We must retrace our steps when we lose our keys or something valuable. We only find it when we go backward. Sometimes, we must go back to a place of simplicity and faith to rekindle the flames of our relationship with God.

God spoke, and Jacob received His word. He didn't run from the voice of God or make excuses; he didn't hide behind the fig leaves of his imagination. Despite the shame of his past, Jacob listened and obeyed, allowing God's word to provide new direction and purpose.

Upon receiving this word, Jacob immediately exercised his authority. He commanded his household to *"put away the strange gods that are among you, and be clean, and change your garments"* (**Gen. 35:2**). In doing so, he embraced his role as king and priest of his home, removing the false gods that had clung to them, perhaps including those of Rachel. It was time to wash away the filth of their past and don new garments, reflecting their new identity (**Romans 13:12-14; Eph. 4:21-24; Col. 3:8, 9**).

As Jacob buried the false gods, God caused terror to fall on the cities around them, ensuring their safety: *"A terror from God fell upon the cities that were around them, so that they did not pursue the sons of Jacob"* (**Gen. 35:5**). When we rid ourselves of demonic influences and depart from idolatry, God can unleash His power against our enemies. Exercising our authority invites God to exercise His. When we fear God more than our idols, our enemies will fear us. We should never hesitate to exercise spiritual authority; instead, we should fear not doing so.

Jacob then refocused his life of worship and obedience by building an altar to the Lord at Bethel. This act deepened his relationship and revelation of God. The first time he was there, he named the place *"the house of God"* (**Gen. 28:17-19**). Now, he shifts his focus from what God does to who God is, naming the altar **"El-Bethel"** – *"The God of the House of God."* Jacob transformed from a man with an experience of God to one with a relationship with God.

The Lord appeared to Jacob and reminded him of his new name and identity: *"Your name is Jacob; no longer shall your name be called Jacob, but Israel shall be your name"* (**Gen. 35:9**). Jacob needed this affirmation to understand that his mistakes and lack of focus had not disqualified him from God's plan and purpose.

He had forgotten why he was alive while searching for a place to settle. God called Jacob to remember his identity as Israel.

Jacob needed to be reminded that he was no longer just Jacob. He had to stop acting like the heel and deceiver he once was and start living as Israel, the one who struggles and prevails with God. This transformation required him to embrace his identity in God as the only proper place of rest. Jacob needed to hear God again affirm, "*You are Israel.*"

In this moment, God revealed Himself to Jacob in a new way, proclaiming Himself as "*God Almighty*" (**El-Shaddai**). The Lord confirmed that the promises made to Abraham and Isaac about the land now belonged to Jacob (**Gen. 35:12**). Jacob responded by setting up a pillar and anointing it, naming it "**Bethel.**"

This renewal of his life led to a renewal of his worship, as Jacob repeated his faith actions to honor the God who called and blessed him. His transformation journey was marked by a deepening relationship with God, reflecting his new identity and purpose.

Lessons for change

- God is faithful, even when we are not. The Bible is a record of God's faithfulness to an unfaithful people. God is always the Father running to his prodigal son. God is always waiting to forgive us and restore us. God will never slam the door in our faces. The Bible says, '*If we confess our sins, he is faithful and just to forgive us our sins and cleanse us from all unrighteousness.*" (**1 John 1:9**). He is faithful. We can come to Him. We can trust Him when we cannot even trust ourselves.

- Identity is the basis of changed behavior. When Jacob encounters God as Bethel, God again reminds Jacob that he is now Israel. God makes us a new person in Christ, and the power of a new lifestyle comes with birth. The essence of the Christian life is to become who we are. The problem is that we have been Jacob so long that we have forgotten that we are now Israel.

- We can live a changed life only because we are a changed person. We can live a changed life because we are now connected to Jesus by the Spirit. Jacob became Israel because God let him win when he wrestled with God. God allowed Jacob to stay connected, and Jacob stayed connected to the Lord until he received the blessing of a new name and identity.

- When we sin, God is still faithful. Even when we relax our grip on God, He never lets us go. Jacob messed up. But Jacob is still Israel. Our failure does not destroy our connection with Christ when we fail God. The prodigal son was always a son, even when he was a prodigal. Every time we walk back to God, we will find Him running to us. (**Luke 15:20**). Our sin does not destroy our identity as a child of God.

- Change does not happen without the exercise of authority. Jacob hears a word from God and takes authority over his life and his family. He removes the idols from the household. They change their garments. They leave their place that was "**towards the city**" and return to Bethel. God did not send an angel to remove the idols. That was Jacob's responsibility.

God does not remove the idols. Jacob takes authority over his life and removes the idols from his household. He treats them as "**dead**" and buries them under a tree.

- God gives us a level of authority to use so we can take responsibility for our lives. We will never change until we exercise authority over what God has given us. We take authority by first taking responsibility. We are responsible for what we think, feel, say, and do. We are accountable for our thoughts, emotions, and actions. Jacob did not blame others for his situation. Jacob took authority and changed what needed to be changed. As we stated earlier, *"If we confess our sins, he is faithful and just to forgive our sins and cleanse us from all unrighteousness."* (**1 John 1:9**). Confession of sins is taking responsibility for them. They are not just "**sins**" but "**our sins.**" No one else is responsible for them. Jesus can only cleanse us from sins we commit and confess, not sins we blame on others.

- Confessing is the first part of responsibility. Jacob did not just admit to having idols but treated them as dead. He changed his clothes to signify they were different people now. This is an Old Testament type of New Testament reality in our spiritual walk with God. The apostle Paul uses the metaphor of changing our clothes as a picture of Christina's discipleship. Paul says that based on our new identity in Christ, *"...put off the old self with its practices, and have put on the self, which is being renewed in knowledge after the image of its creator."* (**Col. 3:9,10. See also Eph. 4: 22-24**). We shed our past behaviors, like we change our clothing.

We do not just confess our sins; we remove sins from our lives as we meet God, just as Jacob did at Bethel.

CHAPTER 12

Loss

"So Rachel died and was buried on the way to Ephrath (Bethlehem)." **(Gen. 35:19.)**

Change is not something that only happens within us; it also happens to us. Relationships once integral to our lives may be taken away or left behind. Some relationships we choose to leave behind to pursue our purpose in God, while others, which we cherish, may be taken from us—either through death or circumstances beyond our control. In just twenty-one verses, **(Gen. 35: 16-29)** Jacob experiences significant losses: the death of the woman who raised him, the woman he loved, and his father, Isaac. He also suffers the betrayal of his firstborn son, Reuben, who sleeps with his concubine, Bilhah. Each of these losses prepares Jacob for the eventual loss of Joseph, his favorite son.

The Bible shows us that these painful losses occur while Jacob pursues God. As he returns to Bethel, God reestablishes their relationship, affirming that Jacob is not just Jacob but Israel **(Gen. 35:10)**. Although Jacob's relationship with God strengthens, he simultaneously endures the loss of those he loves most. We are not exempt from suffering, but our relationship with God is not hindered by heart-wrenching loss.

The Bible doesn't state that we must suffer to grow in God, but it does promise that we are not alone in our suffering. Christ suffers with us because He is in us. The Spirit of the Christ who endured the cross lives within us **(Gal. 2:20)**. Jacob suffered, yet he did not suffer alone; God was with him, and the same God is with us in our suffering.

Deborah

The mention of Deborah's death in (**Genesis 35:8**) is indeed poignant. It seems strategically placed between significant moments of renewal and transformation in Jacob's life. This placement highlights the reality that even amidst profound spiritual experiences, we can face deep personal loss.

As Rebekah's nurse, Deborah represented a strong maternal connection for Jacob. Her passing not only signifies the end of a cherished relationship but also underscores the theme of loss that accompanies change. Jacob's journey back to Bethel, a place of renewal and reconnection with God, is marked by the grief of losing someone who played a vital role in his early life.

This juxtaposition serves as a reminder that life's journey is often intertwined with blessings and sorrows. It reflects the complexity of human experience—how we can experience growth and renewal while simultaneously mourning the loss of someone significant.

God's inclusion of this moment in the narrative shows that He cares about our losses in the grand scheme of our spiritual journeys, no matter how small they seem. It illustrates that Jacob is receiving new blessings and is also processing grief, affirming that God is with us in our joys and sorrows. This truth can resonate deeply with us, reminding us that our emotional experiences are valid and significant in our faith journey.

People who may not seem unique or essential can be significant to God. The death of Deborah is placed amidst the recorded revelations received by Jacob. Could this relationship be just as substantial to Jacob as a word from God? Are there relationships outside of blood relations in our lives that God considers crucial and essential to His love and plan for us?

Did Deborah know she would be included in God's story? Did she realize her life was so important that her passing would be recorded for generations? Does anyone truly understand how significant they are to those around them? We should treasure and nurture these relationships in our lives and strive to be a "**Deborah**" in the lives of others.

Rachel

"Then they journeyed from Bethel. When they were still far from Ephrath, Rachel went into labor and had hard labor. And when her labor was at its hardest, the midwife said to her, '*Do not fear, for you have another son.*' And as her soul was departing *for she was dying*, she called his name Ben-oni, but his father called him Benjamin. So Rachel died and was buried on the way to Ephrath (**Bethlehem**), and Jacob set up a pillar over her tomb. It is the pillar of Rachel's tomb, which is there to this day." (**Gen. 35:16-20**).

In the midst of his spiritual renewal, Jacob loses the love of his life. Rachel was the woman he dreamed of for seven years and then worked another seven years to marry. She was the center of his struggle and desire. Now, as she dies giving birth to their second son, Jacob faces profound loss.

In her final moments, Rachel names her son "**Ben-oni**," meaning "*son of my sorrow.*" However, Jacob refuses to allow his son to be defined by sorrow. He renames him "**Benjamin**," which means "*son of my right hand.*" This act demonstrates that Jacob's faith shines through his broken heart, even in his darkest hour. He declares a future filled with strength and purpose for his son rather than one overshadowed by pain. Rachel may have died, but Jacob's faith and hope lived on.

Rachel dies "*on the way to Ephrath* (**Bethlehem**)." She symbolizes the deep yearning to give birth to God's purpose in one's life. Rachel desires children more than anything and ultimately sacrifices her life to bring forth Benjamin. The tribe of Benjamin would go on to give Israel her first king, Saul, as well as one of history's most significant figures, the apostle Paul, who authored a third of the New Testament. Rachel's legacy includes Joseph, who played a crucial role in preserving the family of God and many nations. Yet, Rachel is connected to an even greater birth: she died on the way to Bethlehem, where Christ was born.

The Gospel of Matthew recounts Jesus' birth in Bethlehem, where King Herod, in a desperate attempt to eliminate the Messiah, ordered the slaughter of all male infants. This tragic event fulfills Micah's prophecy, declaring Bethlehem as the birthplace of the Messiah. Additionally, the prophet Jeremiah foretold that the cries of Rachel, who died en route to Bethlehem, would echo as a prophetic lament for the slain children. Rachel's story intertwines with the profound narrative of hope and sorrow, ultimately pointing to the coming of Christ and the sacrifice inherent in the journey of faith.

"*A voice was heard in Ramah, weeping and loud lamentation. Rachel weeping for her children: She refused to be comforted because they are no more.*" (**Mat. 2:18,** referring to **Jer. 31:15**).

The death of Rachel on the way to Bethlehem serves as a poignant reminder that birthing something new often comes at a significant cost. In our journeys, we will inevitably face both burials and births. Rachel's passing underscores the importance of having faith even in the depths of pain and suffering. Jacob re-named his son, Benjamin, refusing to let him bear the weight of sorrow and death. Despite the darkness of loss, life ultimately triumphed; Herod's attempts to eliminate Jesus failed, as death could not hold Him. In the end, when death did confront Jesus, it was defeated forever.

Throughout his life, Jacob marked significant moments with pillars, each one representing a profound change. He erected a pillar at Bethel when he first encountered God (**Gen. 28:18**), another upon returning (**Gen. 35:14**), and a third to signify his separation from Laban (**Gen. 31:51**). After Rachel's death, he again erected a pillar (**Gen. 35:20**), memorializing a moment that would forever alter his life.

The loss of a loved one profoundly impacts us, and Jacob carried the weight of Rachel's absence throughout his life, recalling her during the blessing of their grandchildren, Ephraim and Manasseh (**Gen. 48:7**). It's vital to mark these moments of loss, as they shape our journeys. However, these pillars should serve as markers, not mansions; they should remind us of our past while allowing us to move forward.

While cemeteries, meaning *"places of memory,"* are essential for honoring those we've lost, we must not dwell there like the Gadarene demoniac (**Mark 5:3**). Jacob honored Rachel and loved her deeply. Yet, he did not allow his grief to halt his journey of faith. In our lives, we should strive to do the same, recognizing that while loss is painful, it does not have to define our path.

Reuben

"While Israel lived in that land, Reuben went and lay with Bilhah, his father's concubine. And Israel heard of it." (**Gen. 35:22**).

The worst pain someone can experience outside of death is betrayal, and Reuben's act of dishonor and rebellion against Jacob was profound. By sleeping with Bilhah, his father's concubine,

Reuben committed a grave offense—not just a sexual sin but a significant challenge to his father's authority. This act was akin to claiming the patriarch's power for himself, as seen later with Absalom's similar actions against David (**2 Sam. 16:20-23**).

As the firstborn son, Reuben held the potential for a double portion of the inheritance (**Deut. 21:17**). Yet, in his impatience, he disqualified himself and his lineage from receiving a meaningful inheritance. Notably, the text refers to Jacob as "**Israel**" in this context. Reuben's betrayal was not merely against Jacob as a father but against the covenantal relationship that Jacob represented.

Jacob's response to this betrayal was silence; he did nothing when learning about Reuben's actions. However, this betrayal lingered in Jacob's mind. Reuben was notably excluded on his deathbed when he blessed his sons. The last word Jacob spoke to Reuben was one of severe consequence, highlighting the lasting impact of betrayal on both personal and covenantal levels. *"Reuben, you are my firstborn, my might, and the first fruits of my strength, preeminent in dignity and power. Unstable as water, you shall not have preeminence because you went up to your father's bed; then you defiled it—he went up to my couch! "* (**Gen. 49:3,4**).

The mention of Reuben and his betrayal here in this cluster of losses shows us that the death of a relationship can be as traumatic as the death of a person. Betrayal is an intentional act of harm against us by someone in a loving and loyal relationship. Betrayal is more painful than death because a person does not want to die. Still, they are fully invested in the betrayal of your relationship. Jacob endured the pain of betrayal and the loss of a relationship for many years. Jacob would eventually be betrayed by almost all his sons in their actions against Joseph.

Jacob did not allow the pain of betrayal to stop him from his journey of faith and change with God. It seems that the name "**Israel**," used here instead of just "**Jacob**," tells us that Jacob carried this pain as Israel, not as Jacob. He carried his pain in the strength of his covenant relationship with God. We must remember that no matter who betrays us, the Lord will never betray us (**Ps. 27:10; 41:9-12**). We need to remember that Jesus knows the pain of betrayal well. Judas sold him for thirty pieces of silver, Peter denied Him, and the other disciples besides John could not be found near Him at the cross. Betrayal was a heavy weight of pain that Jesus bore on the cross. We also need to remember that the same One who carried the betrayal of love conquered betrayal as He conquered death. The Resurrected Lord lives in us so that while we carry the pain of death and betrayal, we are also "more than conquerors" over this pain. Just as the wounds of the crucifixion were incorporated into the Risen Christ, we can also rise above our wounds to become everything God has called us to be.

Isaac

"And Jacob came to his Father's house at Mamre, or Kiriath-Arba (Hebron), where Abraham and Isaac had sojourned. Now, the days of Isaac were 180 years. And Isaac breathed his last, died, and was gathered to his people, old and full of days. And his sons Esau and Jacob buried him." (**Gen, 35:27-29**)

When Rachel died, Jacob returned to Hebron, where his family was buried, and simply "**came to his father.**" The text offers no account of a joyous reunion—no "waiting father" rushing to embrace a son who had been away for twenty years. Jacob came home, and shortly after, Isaac died.

Sometimes, stories conclude without proper closure. Relationships may end without the healing or reconciliation we hope for, leaving unresolved emotions buried deep. We may say **"goodbye,"** but it doesn't always feel good.

Yet there's a poignant moment: *"his sons Esau and Jacob buried him."* In that moment, the estranged brothers unite one last time to honor their father. Isaac remained in the Promised Land, a seed offered to God, now laid to rest in the land that awaited harvest. The next chapter in the Bible focuses on Esau and his descendants. At the same time, the narrative continues with Jacob and his lineage.

In that moment of burial, the twin brothers, who once battled for their birthright, set aside their differences to pay their respects. They were simply two boys who loved their father. Despite their complex histories, they both move forward to fulfill Isaac's imparted destinies.

Lessons for change

- Our pursuit of God does not exempt us from the pains of life. Death comes to us all. Paul said believers do *"not grieve as others do, who have no hope."* (**1 Thes. 4:13**). But that does not mean we do not grieve. Jesus raised Lazarus from the tomb, but He still wept. (**John 11:35**). One-third of the Psalms in the Bible are laments, songs of grief and loss written as hymns of praise and worship to the God who comforts and holds us. We bury our loved ones, but we should not bury our grief. We learn to carry our wounds. Jesus rose from the dead but could still show His wounds (**John 20:27**). We integrate grief into our lives and have the scars of heartache and betrayal in the power of the Resurrection to minister to others (**2 Cor. 1:3,4**).

- We should never allow anything to stop us from our journey of change. Rachel died, and Jacob erected a pillar. But he did not stop. Reuben, his first-born son, betrayed him. He did not stop. Things happen that will break our hearts, but they must not stop our journey. Have we let a tragedy de-rail us from our journey?

- Following Jesus means following Jesus. Every pain of death and betrayal that we face has already been faced by Him. He conquered all, and through Him, *"we are more than conquerors through Him who loved us."* (**Romans 8:37**). Jesus said following Him was taking our cross daily and following Him (**Luke 9:23**). We do not stop in our suffering; we carry our suffering and transform the world with what forms us to the image of His Son. We should understand that we must first change ourselves to change the world. Before every resurrection, there is first a cross.

CHAPTER 13

Revival

"Jacob's journey to Egypt marks a pivotal moment in the narrative. When his sons finally tell him that Joseph is alive and is a ruler in Egypt, Jacob's heart is initially numb with disbelief. However, Jacob's spirit revives as they recount Joseph's words and show him the wagons sent by Joseph. He joyfully declares, "It is enough; Joseph, my son, is still alive. I will go and see him before I die."

Before setting out, Jacob stops at Beersheba to offer sacrifices to God. In a decisive encounter, God calls to him at night, identifying Himself as "the God of your father." He reassures Jacob, telling him not to fear going to Egypt, promising that He will make Jacob a great nation there and that He will accompany him. God assures Jacob that Joseph will be with him until the end.

With renewed purpose and confidence, Jacob embarks on his journey. His sons carry him, their families, and their possessions in the wagons Pharaoh sent, marking a significant transition for the entire family. They bring everything into Egypt, highlighting a physical relocation and the beginning of a new chapter in their collective story, rooted in God's promises and blessings. **(Gen. 45:25-46:4).**

The latter chapters of Genesis shift focus from Jacob's tumultuous life to the dramatic saga of Joseph and his brothers. Jacob, still profoundly affected by his past losses, favors Joseph, giving him a richly ornamented coat, symbolizing his unique status and authority within the family. Jacob does not anticipate the following devastating events when he sends Joseph to check on his brothers.

The brothers betray Joseph, selling him into slavery and later presenting Jacob with the bloody coat, leading him to believe that his beloved son is dead. Jacob's grief is profound and prolonged; he mourns for years, unable to accept the truth that Joseph is still alive.

Meanwhile, the narrative reveals Joseph's trials and eventual rise to power in Egypt—his unjust imprisonment, his interpretations of dreams, and his ascendance to a position of authority. However, Jacob remains in the dark about Joseph's fate, believing him to be lost forever.

As famine strikes the land, Jacob is forced to send his sons to Egypt for help. They return with news that a powerful ruler has accused them of being spies and that Simeon is being held as collateral until they return with Benjamin. Initially, Jacob refuses to let Benjamin go, clinging to the last remnant of Rachel. Still, as the famine worsens, he has no choice but to relent.

Finally, the sons return with extraordinary news: "*Joseph is alive! He is the ruler of Egypt, and he wants us to come live near him.*" The joy of this revelation brings Jacob's spirit back to life, igniting hope and a desire to reunite with the son he thought he had lost forever. This turning point marks a significant transformation for Jacob as he prepares to embrace a new chapter of his life, filled with the possibility of reconciliation and restoration.

Good News. Broken Heart.

When Jacob's sons first shared the astonishing news that Joseph was alive and a ruler in Egypt, he responded with disbelief: "*Jacob's heart became numb, for he did not believe them*" (**Gen. 45:26**). This reaction highlights the profound impact of his long-standing grief. While his mind processed the information, his heart remained closed off, encased in layers of sorrow and depression that had built up over the years since Joseph's supposed death.

Once vibrant and full of hope, Jacob's heart had been shattered by loss. A broken heart often becomes numb and hardened, resisting the possibility of further pain. In Jacob's case, accepting good news felt risky; he feared another heartbreak might be more than he could bear. This fear can cause us to reject hope as we convince ourselves that it's safer to remain in the familiar darkness of despair than to risk disappointment.

For Jacob, the revelation that Joseph was alive represented a profound shift in his reality. Yet, he struggled to embrace this new truth without changing his heart. The emotional scars from past losses made it difficult for him to open up to the possibility of joy again. Sometimes, we resist good news simply because it feels too good to be true, and the prospect of opening ourselves up again feels overwhelmingly daunting. Jacob's experience serves as a reminder that healing takes time and that we must allow ourselves to feel, even when it's painful, to indeed receive the blessings that await us.

The Breakthrough

This truth began to penetrate Jacob's broken heart through two key factors: his sons' persistent verbal testimony and the wagons' undeniable presence. Despite his reasons for skepticism—given Reuben's betrayal and Simeon and Levi's violent actions—Jacob's sons continued to insist that Joseph was alive and well. Their unwavering commitment to their story, reinforced even by Benjamin's participation, slowly began to chip away at Jacob's doubts.

The pivotal moment came when Jacob saw the wagons. Seeing such valuable vehicles provided undeniable evidence that something extraordinary was happening. The wagons were too lavish to have been stolen, and if his sons had fabricated this tale, there would be no motive for them to return to Egypt. The logical conclusion was clear: Joseph was alive, a ruler in Egypt, and he wanted Jacob and his family to join him.

Jacob's heart began to revive as hope surged through him. The prospect of reuniting with Joseph brought a light to his dark world that he hadn't felt in years. He was no longer just a grieving father; he was on the brink of a new chapter, filled with the promise of restoration and the joy of family.

Revival

The text notes that *"the spirit of their father revived."* This word **"revived"** resonates deeply, echoing the moment in Ezekiel when God promises to breathe life into a valley of dry bones, bringing them back to life (**Ezek. 37:5**). For Jacob, the good news of Joseph's survival pierced through the layers of grief that had numbed his heart, much like the breath of God rejuvenating those lifeless bones.

In Ezekiel's vision, the valley symbolizes utter despair and death, where hope seems irretrievably lost. Yet, God instructs Ezekiel to prophesy to the bones, urging them to hear His word. As Ezekiel obeys, those dry bones come to life, forming an exceedingly great army (**Ezek. 37:1-14**). This mirrors Jacob's experience; the announcement of Joseph's survival revitalizes his spirit, reigniting hope where there had been only despair.

Many of us find ourselves in similar valleys, believing that the opportunity for change and transformation has passed us by. We might feel too old, wounded, or entrenched in our pain to embrace hope. The idea of light piercing our darkness can feel painful, and we might be tempted to stay numb, accustomed to our suffering.

Yet, just as Jacob heard the life-changing news, we too can encounter words of hope. We might read something that stirs our hearts or listen to testimonies of transformation that reignite our belief in the possibility of change. The gospel reminds us that Jesus not only died for our sins but was resurrected, offering us new life. The same power that raised Him from the dead is available to us.

As we witness the changes in others—addictions broken, marriages restored, health renewed—we begin to believe that God has not given up on us. We open ourselves to the possibility that He wants to breathe new life into our dry bones. What was once broken can be healed, and what was lost can be found again. Through faith, we can reclaim our identity and embrace the revival that God desires for us.

Renewal

Jacob was transformed by the good news. Notice the name change in the text: "*...the spirit of their father Jacob revived. And Israel said, 'It is enough; Joseph is still alive. I will go and see him before I die'*" (**Gen. 45:28**). His name shifts from Jacob to Israel once again. Years earlier, Jacob had emerged from a struggle in the dark and was changed from Jacob to Israel. Now, after years of darkness, he becomes Israel again. Jacob received the good news, and it renewed his identity.

This name change signifies a renewal of the heart and a reaffirmation of his covenant with God. Jacob is revitalized to follow the God who has called him. As Israel, he responds to the good news and sets out to see Joseph.

"So Israel took his journey with all that he had, came to Beersheba, and offered sacrifices to the God of his father, Isaac. And God spoke to Israel in visions of the night and said, 'Jacob, Jacob.' And he said, 'Here I am.' Then He said, 'I am God, the God of your father. Do not be afraid to go down to Egypt; I will make you a great nation there. I will go down with you to Egypt and bring you up again, and Joseph's hand shall close your eyes.'" (**Gen. 46:1-4**)

Jacob is referred to as Israel during this journey, emphasizing his transformed identity. Before leaving the land promised to Abraham and Isaac, Jacob stops at Beersheba to offer sacrifices *"to the God of his father, Isaac."* Beersheba marks the last point before departing from the Promised Land. Abraham had gone to Egypt, but when he returned, he never left the land again. Jacob appears to be abandoning the covenant promise as he prepares to leave.

Jacob prays to the **"God of Isaac,"** recognizing that Isaac remained faithful to the land, digging wells and laboring there without leaving. Jacob seems concerned that he may be unfaithful to the promise by embarking on this new journey. He stops to worship on the border, seeking assurance that leaving the land does not mean abandoning the promise.

The Lord speaks to Jacob *"in the visions of the night"* (**Gen. 46:2**), calling his name twice: **"Jacob, Jacob."** This mirrors how God addressed Abraham, providing reassurance that Jacob did not need to fear going down to Egypt. God assured him that He would accompany him and that Jacob would eventually return with Joseph by his side.

Jacob seeks this assurance because he stands at the threshold of the promise, haunted by the falsehood of Joseph's death and wary of the truth of his survival. In our journeys, we often face **"border situations"** where the path forward is unclear. In such times, we must be sensitive to the Holy Spirit's guidance, as there may not always be specific biblical principles that apply to our circumstances.

The Bible tells us, *"For as many as are led by the Spirit of God, they are the sons of God"* (**Romans 8:14**). In our lives, we frequently need specific direction. We risk missing God if we do not remain open to His voice through any means He chooses.

Lessons for change

- It is the good news of the Gospel that brings change. *"Christ died for our sins, following the Scriptures, that he was buried, that he was raised on the third day following the Scriptures."* (**1 Cor. 15:3,4**). What many churches today preach is good advice, not good news. We do not hear that *"Christ was raised from the dead by the glory of the Father, that we should walk in newness of life"* (**Rom. 6:4**). We hear principles of self-help, nuggets of human wisdom garnished with Scripture and songs to motivate us to get through and keep going. Good advice is not enough. We must embrace the gospel as the good news of the kingdom of God as Jesus preached and lived. We must understand that the good news is that we go to heaven, and heaven has come to earth. Dry bones can live again because Jesus conquered death, and His life can now be in us.

- We need to preach with words and with wagons. Jacob believed because of what his sons said and because of the wagons. Jesus said, *"If I am not doing the works of my Father, then do not believe me; but if I do them, even if you do not believe me, believe the works, that you may know and understand that the Father is in me, and I am in the Father."* (**John 10:37,38**). Jesus loves it when we receive the promises of God without the need for signs. Still, He welcomes those who also need convincing evidence to believe. (John 20:29). We need words and wagons. We need the ministry of signs, wonders, and miracles in the church because many have broken and damaged hearts that are so lost that they need many signs before they can find their way back to God. The wagons were not sent as a sign. The wagons were sent to do a job and fulfill a need, but they became a sign to Jacob that the good news was confirmed. Likewise, Jesus did not heal people, so they would believe. Jesus healed people because He came to make men whole. But those healings and miracles caused people to think the good news of the Kingdom. The good news of the Kingdom still needs to be proclaimed, and the power of the Kingdom is still available to those who seek healing and deliverance.

- Persistence is essential to change. The sons did not give up telling Jacob the excellent news. His heart could not receive it at first. It took time. The Bible says that through **"faith and patience,"** we inherit the promises of God (**Heb. 6:12**). Do not let the pain of the past stop the Word from being preached. People need time to think about the **"wagons"** that God sends them in their life. Healing of broken hearts is not always instantaneous. Healing is often a process that requires persistence and patience. We know that the same Jesus that conquered death, hell, and the grave can break through and heal every broken heart and life. Keep speaking the Word.

CHAPTER 14

Generational Change

"After this, Joseph was told, "Behold, your father is ill." So he took with him his two sons, Manasseh and Ephraim. And Jacob was told, "Your son Joseph has come to you." Then Israel summoned his strength and sat up in bed. And Jacob said to Joseph, "God Almighty appeared to me at Luz in the land of Canaan and blessed me, and said to me, 'Behold, I will make you fruitful and multiply you, and I will make of you a company of peoples and will give this land to your offspring after you for an everlasting possession.' And now your two sons, who were born to you in the land of Egypt before I came to you in Egypt, are mine; Ephraim and Manasseh shall be mine, as Reuben and Simeon are. And the children that you fathered after them shall be yours. They shall be called by the name of their brothers in their inheritance. As for me, when I came from Paddan to my sorrow, Rachel died in the land of Canaan on the way when there was still some distance to go to Ephrath, and I buried her there on the way to Ephrath "that is, Bethlehem."" (Gen. 48:1-7)

Change is not just about transforming our lives; it's about changing generations. The changes in Jacob's life have echoed through centuries, impacting countless lives. When we experience transformation, we're altering our destiny and that of our children and grandchildren. God promised Abraham, *"I will make of thee a great nation, and I will bless thee, and make thy name great; and thou shalt be a blessing"* (**Gen. 12:2**). This promise was reiterated to Jacob: *"In thy seed shall all the families of the earth be blessed"* (**Gen. 28:14**). God's intention in our lives isn't solely for our benefit; it's to enable us to be a blessing to others. What God is doing in us can create an avalanche of blessings and grace, rolling through the years to bring hope and change to future generations.

Testimony

Joseph brings his two sons, Manasseh and Ephraim, to Jacob, knowing that time is running out for the blessing to be passed on. Before Jacob lays his hands upon them, he shares his testimony, recounting how he encountered God at Bethel: *"God Almighty appeared to me at Luz in the land of Canaan and blessed me..."* (**Gen. 48:3,4**).

Jacob then declares that he has adopted Ephraim and Manasseh, elevating them to the status of tribes of their own. This grants Joseph the double portion of the firstborn son, as his two sons are now considered equal to Jacob's other sons: *"And now your two sons, who were born to you in the land of Egypt before I came to Egypt, are mine. Ephraim and Manasseh shall be mine, as Reuben and Simeon are"* (**Gen. 48:5**).

To complete his testimony, Jacob reflects on the death of Rachel, Joseph's mother. He recounts, *"As for me when I came from Paddan to my sorrow Rachel died in the land of Canaan on the way, when there was still some distance to go to Ephrath, and I buried her there on the way to Ephrath (that is, Bethlehem)."* By sharing his story of blessing and pain, Jacob imparts a grace that enriches Ephraim and Manasseh, connecting them to their heritage and the love he holds for their mother.

One of the ways to impact the next generation is to tell your story. The very center of the worship of the Tabernacle was a piece of furniture called **"the Ark of the Covenant."** This Ark, which was kept in the Most Holy Place behind the veil, contained the powerful presence of God. It was also known as *"the Ark of* *the Testimony*" (**Ex. 25:22**), symbolizing the covenant's significance. When we carry our testimony, we take the presence of God. Sharing what He has done for us can impart faith and grace, blessing those who listen.

Atop the Ark was the mercy seat, where God met with His people (**Ex. 30:6**). When we share our testimonies of grace and mercy, we invite that divine encounter. Our stories can be seeds for the next great harvest.

Blessing the Generations

Like Abraham and Isaac before him, Jacob struggled to receive his birthright and blessing. He spent twenty years exiled from the land of promise and wrestled with God and man to walk in his blessing. That's why Jacob doesn't just testify about his encounter with God but also about the burial of Rachel. He buried her on the way to Bethlehem, the future birthplace of Jesus. The next generation needs to understand that we often bury something before the birth of a blessing.

As Jacob prepares to lay hands-on Joseph's sons, his testimony reflects that this blessing comes from God but also through a painful price. Jacob paid dearly for the blessings in his life. Joseph's sons were alive because their father, Joseph, had paid a heavy price to walk in integrity and grace, enduring years of slavery and imprisonment. How many tears were shed during those decades of loneliness and abandonment? How many years did Jacob limp through a broken heart while Joseph served without hope in sight? And yet, Ephraim and Manasseh simply walk into the blessing.

We receive blessings of grace that we did not earn; someone else paid the price for them. We are saved by grace through faith, but our redemption was secured by the precious blood of Jesus (**1 Peter 1:19**). Even in the natural world, we who have never fought in a war enjoy the freedom that was paid for by those who sacrificed in battle. This is why the Lord leads us through trials and experiences—not just to change us but to accelerate blessings as we share and impart our stories to the next generation. If you pass on your experiences, they can start where you left off, leading to a multiplication of blessings instead of mere additions. Your pain can become their gain.

Intention

When Joseph presents his sons to Jacob, he places his firstborn on Jacob's right side and the second son on his left, following the natural order of inheritance. However, Jacob crosses his hands and places his right hand on the younger son. Joseph, thinking his father has made a mistake due to poor eyesight, tries to correct him. But Jacob reassures him, saying, "*I know it, my son, I know it*" (**Gen. 48:19**). Jacob's lack of eyesight does not equate to a lack of insight; he intentionally follows the spiritual order of blessing the younger son.

Blessing never happens by accident. If you don't actively seek to pass your blessing to the next generation, it simply won't occur. Your children and grandchildren won't absorb grace just because you've received it from the Lord. You must live with intention and purpose, allowing God to change you and placing your children and grandchildren in line to receive. The blessing comes not by your hand but through your hands. God has entrusted you with people in your generations, whether by blood or spiritual ties, and they will not be blessed unless you bless them. Jacob knew what he was doing and intentionally blessed the next generation. Do we?

Before his death, Jacob blesses his sons, and Genesis 49 is filled with blessings—words that will become garments of praise and identity for his sons and their descendants for generations to come. We need to speak and bless others with faith and intention. Our words will outlive us, creating a bridge for the next generation to navigate the barriers they face. Jacob left a legacy of words for his children, and so should we.

Legacy

The writer of Hebrews states, *"By faith Jacob, when dying, blessed each of the sons of Joseph, bowing in worship over the head of his staff"* (**Hebrews 11:21**). Jacob's staff symbolizes his pilgrimage and wanderings. When he prayed to the Lord for preservation from Esau, he referenced his staff: *"I am not worthy of the least of all the mercies, and of all the truth, which thou hast showed unto thy servant; for with my staff I passed over this Jordan; and now I have become two bands"* (**Gen. 32:10**). The only thing Jacob brought from his days in Isaac's household was his staff, which he carried from the vision at Bethel, through years with Laban, back into the Promised Land, and down into Egypt.

It's said that men of this time carved symbols and words of remembrance into their staffs, making each one unique and filled with the markings of their memories. Jacob, *"bowing in worship over the head of his staff,"* worshipped the Lord at the pinnacle of his journey in faith.

In worship, we lean on what the Lord has done. Jacob's staff was filled with blessings and brokenness, miracles and mayhem, promises and pain. He worshipped because God had brought him through it all. When Jacob first carried the staff, his name meant **"heel"** and **"trickster."** Now, he has the new name **"Israel,"** symbolizing his struggle with man and God—and his victory. God remained faithful to His promises, and Jacob was forever changed. He left home with a staff and entered Egypt with 75 souls. They would someday leave Egypt as a mighty nation. Through Jacob's transformation, God changed the world.

Jacob worshipped as he approached death. We never know what God might do through us. While we all leave this world, not everyone changes it. Jacob made an impact because God changed him. To leave a legacy, we must become a blessing to future generations, sharing what the Lord has given us. And that change starts with us.

Lessons for change

- Our change provides a generational inheritance in the Spirit. The Bible says, *"A good man leaves an inheritance to his children's children..."*. (**Prov. 13:22**). This does not refer to finances alone. This means that when we are changed by Jesus, that blessing will affect the generations. Jacob never thought he would ever see Joseph again. Not only did he see Joseph again, but he was also able to bless his children. You never know the surprise that awaits us when we discover how our journey of change also changed the lives of generations after us. This should encourage us to persevere during sadness and grief because our trip is never about us.
- We must share our **"test"** when we share our **"testimony."** Grief is not something we **"get over."** Grief is something we incorporate into our lives.

Jacob, even at his death, is still thinking about Rachel. He remembers when and where he buried her. Her death is part of his story, his testimony to the next generations. Our testimony in Christ is not always the good news of what we escaped from but the good news of what He brought us through. Those who follow the Lord must know that the journey will have blessings and burials. Sharing our grief is not grievous to others. We need to share a part of our life with God.

- We always worship at the top of our staff. Worship is fueled by the fire of God and kept aflame by stirring up the memories of his faithfulness. If we ever feel the fire of enthusiasm waning in our lives, we must look at everything God has said and done for us. We should not wait until we are at the end of our journey to praise Him. The Lord has already brought us through more than we can ever know or share. And He will never stop loving and blessing us. He is worthy of our praise!